STORY
Intelligence

In an era where trust is increasingly fragile and AI-generated content is ever-present; this is a must-read for business leaders. Gabrielle is a masterful storyteller and in her new book she explains why authentic human stories are not just important, but essential for cutting through the noise and building genuine connection. This book smartly reframes AI not as a threat, but as an incredibly powerful creative partner, showing how we can use it to amplify and strengthen any story that needs to be heard.

—**Michelle Hutton**, Chief Client Officer, Burson

In a world increasingly dominated by 'thinking machines', Gabrielle Dolan brilliantly reminds us that humans are 'feeling machines that think'. The very title, *Story Intelligence*, signals a vital evolution beyond traditional narrative craft for the age of AI. She guides us not to replace our humanity with technology, but to use it to amplify our uniquely human gift for storytelling. This book is a crucial lesson that logic and data alone will never be enough to truly move people. Dolan's assertion that 'experience is the best teacher, a compelling story is a close second' is a profound truth for any leader looking to inspire action. I recommend this book as essential reading for anyone looking to retain authenticity and connection while mastering modern AI tools.

—**Dr Sue Keay**, Director, University NSW AI Institute

To story is human, but to story for influence requires guidance. *Story Intelligence* shows readers exactly how to craft narratives for maximum impact. If you need this superpower, you need this wonderful book!

—**Paul J. Zak, PhD**, author of *The Little Book of Happiness: A Scientific Approach to Living Better*

Professional storytelling is widely acknowledged as a powerful tool. But is it under threat from AI? *Story Intelligence* convincingly argues that AI is not a threat but a highly effective partner in enhancing storytelling skills. By understanding the core principles of storytelling (succinctly summarised in the book), AI can be harnessed to unlock our creativity. This book is an uplifting and exciting read, especially for those tentative about integrating AI into their creative processes.

—**Maia Gould**, Associate Professor, The Australian National University

As deep tech continues to reshape our everyday and the communication landscape, through synthetic media, and AI-generated misinformation, the need for authentic human storytelling has never been greater. Gabrielle Dolan's *Story Intelligence* is a timely and essential guide for anyone seeking to build trust in a world of manipulated narratives and eroded truth. With Dolan's typical warmth, wit and practical wisdom, she reminds us that while AI can generate words, only humans can tell stories that truly resonate.

—**Prerana Mehta**, CEO, Australian Council of Learned Academies

In a world where executives are told to 'tell their story' but given little guidance on how to do it powerfully, especially when trust in leadership is at an all-time low, this book is the missing piece. Gabrielle's blend of authenticity, storytelling smarts and practical AI strategy is a game changer. Essential reading for those of us helping leaders show up, speak up and shape culture with their voice.

—**Amanda Blesing**, Executive Coach and 3x author for Leading Women

In a world where trust is eroding and attention is fleeting, this book is a timely and powerful reminder of why storytelling matters more than ever. It introduces a compelling new dimension of human capability: Story Intelligence (SQ)—the ability to authentically and purposefully use narrative to connect, engage, and inspire.

Going beyond cognitive intelligence (IQ), emotional intelligence (EQ), and cultural intelligence (CQ), the book makes a bold and original case for SQ as a core human skill—one that not only drives meaningful communication but also fosters deeper connection in an age shaped by technology and cultural fragmentation.

Gabriel skilfully explores how AI can serve as a creative partner in this journey, not by replacing our stories but by helping us uncover and share them more authentically.

This book is insightful, timely, and filled with soul. If you care about meaningful connection in the digital age, this is an absolute must-read. You'll walk away not just thinking differently, but feeling differently—about stories, technology, and about yourself.
—**Dr. Frederique Covington Corbett**, author of *Leadership on a Blockchain* and Chief Global Brand & Marketing, PFP

Story Intelligence is a timely, practical read. If you need to connect with others and build trust (and who doesn't?), this is the book for you. Gabrielle Dolan walks the talk, with real stories, useful tools and a solid case for why authenticity is almost always the answer.
—**Alicia McKay**, author of *You Don't Need An MBA*

Story Intelligence shows us that stories don't just inform, they connect. Gabrielle Dolan reveals how stories cut through logic, tapping into something deeper to build trust, shift thinking and move people. A smart book on the superpower we all carry.
—**Matt Church**, Founder, Thought Leaders Business School and author of *Future Proof Humans*

Gabrielle's best book yet! At last a sensible use of AI to mine human experience and help us connect better with others. The stories shared left me uplifted and motivated, eager to shift my communication in a meaningful way. Pithy and practical, this book will help you double down on authenticity and level up your impact.
—**Zoë Routh**, Leadership futurist and award-winning author

Gabrielle Dolan has done it again—taking something as timeless as storytelling and giving it a fresh, urgent relevance for the world we live in now. In an age where AI content floods our feeds and trust is harder to earn, *Story Intelligence* is the reminder we all need—that our authentic stories are the heartbeat of connection. What I love most is how Gabrielle doesn't frame AI as the villain but as a tool—a creative partner—when used with intention and heart. This book is smart, real and a must-read for anyone who wants to stand out with their true voice, not just more noise.

—**Janine Garner**, author of *Be Brilliant* and *It's Who You Know*

Story Intelligence is a game changer for any leader who wants to deepen connection, influence with authenticity, and leave a lasting impact. Gabrielle Dolan beautifully unpacks the power of storytelling as a strategic tool—not just for communication, but for genuine leadership. If you're ready to elevate your message and engage on a whole new level, this book is your roadmap."

—**Jane Anderson**, Business Growth and Communication Expert

Story Intelligence is a smart, practical guide to elevating your storytelling with AI. Packed with sharp insights and practical takeaways, it's a GPS for modern communicators navigating the new rules of storytelling. A must-read for anyone ready to turn AI into a powerful creative partner.

—**Tennille Burt**, Chief Marketing Officer

This is the story of how to tell stories in an age of algorithms. It's smart, brave, and brimming with integrity.

—**Prof. Catherine Ball**, Scientific Futurist

STORY
Intelligence

THE CRAFT OF
AUTHENTIC STORYTELLING
MADE SMARTER WITH AI

GABRIELLE DOLAN

WILEY

First published 2026 by John Wiley & Sons Australia, Ltd

ISBN: 978-1-394-36087-1

A catalogue record for this book is available from the National Library of Australia

Registered Office
John Wiley & Sons Australia, Ltd. Level 4, 600 Bourke Street, Melbourne, VIC 3000, Australia

For details of our global editorial offices, customer services, and more information about Wiley products visit us at www.wiley.com.

Wiley also publishes its books in a variety of electronic formats and by print-on-demand. Some content that appears in standard print versions of this book may not be available in other formats.

Cover design by Wiley
Cover image: © phochi/Shutterstock

Set in 11.5/15.5pts and Plantin Std by Straive, Chennai, India.
Printed and bound by CPI Group (UK) Ltd, Croydon, CR0 4YY
C9781394360871_131125
The manufacturer's authorized representative according to the EU General Product Safety Regulation is Wiley-VCH GmbH, Boschstr. 12, 69469 Weinheim, Germany, e-mail: Product_Safety@wiley.com.

Contents

About the author

Gabrielle Dolan, affectionately known as 'Ral' to those who've met her, is a globally recognised expert in strategic storytelling and real communication. It was while working in senior leadership roles at National Australia Bank that she discovered how stories could enhance communication and leadership effectiveness.

Since that realisation, Gabrielle has dedicated her career to helping people humanise their communications. She travels the world undertaking storytelling workshops and delivering keynote speeches at conferences, where she is known as an 'edutainer'; that is, someone who educates and entertains.

An accomplished author, Gabrielle has penned seven influential books, including the bestseller *Magnetic Stories: Connect with customers and engage employees with brand storytelling,* which debuted at number two on Australia's best-selling business books list.

She co-hosts a podcast with Jac Phillips called *Keeping it Real with Jac and Ral,* which ranked in the top 5 per cent of video-produced podcasts on Spotify. Gabrielle met Jac over 20 years ago and the relationship went from client, to friend to podcast co-host. Jac is an amazing, no-nonsense leadership coach.

Gabrielle holds a Master's degree in Management and Leadership, an Associate Diploma in Education and Training and is a graduate of the Harvard Kennedy School of Executive Education. Her academic achievements underscore her commitment to continuous learning and leadership development ... or, to potentially making up for not passing English in her final year of high school!

Gabrielle's dedication to clear and genuine business dialogue led her to initiate the global movement Jargon Free Fridays, encouraging professionals to ditch corporate jargon and unnecessary acronyms in favour of straightforward communication. Her efforts were recognised in 2020 when she was named Communicator of the Year by the International Association of Business Communicators Asia–Pacific region.

Gabrielle spends her time between Melbourne and Bermagui on the southern New South Wales coast of Australia. She is married to Steve and they have two adult daughters, Alex and Jess. She is committed to improving her game ... specifically on the golf course and pickleball court.

Introduction

On the eve of Halloween in 1938, 'The War of the Worlds' hit the airwaves on CBS Radio. An adaptation of HG Wells' novel of the same name, which was published 40 years prior, it was directed and narrated by Orsen Welles (no relative of the original author).

Instead of being set in 19th-century England, the episode was changed to the current day in the United States. The hour-long program was a simulation of a normal evening radio broadcast with weather updates and music, but after a few minutes, the music was interrupted by supposedly real news, detailing the beginning of a devastating alien invasion and the United States military's futile efforts to stop it.

One of the so-called 'reports' was from a rooftop in Manhattan, where a news reporter describes the invasion on New York City saying, 'Five great machines wading through the Hudson River like men wading through a brook. There is black smoke drifting over the city and people are diving into the East River like rats, and others in Times Square are falling like flies'. The actor playing this journalist then coughs and collapses. After seconds of silence, a radio operator is heard calling, 'New York. Isn't there anyone on the air? Isn't there anyone on the air? Isn't there…anyone?'

Thousands of listeners missed the start of this broadcast, which actually explained it was fictionalised, and mistakenly took it for genuine news. They believed it to be true and shared the false reports with others, spreading it like wildfire. Chaos ensued as people took to the streets in confusion.

Imagine waking up to that news; what would you think? Fast forward to today, imagine waking up to a video of a world leader heavily criticising another world leader and threatening war, only to find out hours later that it was entirely fabricated. Or seeing a heartfelt testimonial about a product, only to discover that the person speaking doesn't exist.

Sadly, this is no longer just the plot of a dystopian novel acted out for entertainment. It is our reality… right here, right now.

It's impossible not to notice the influx of fake videos on your social media feed… of lions swallowing whole snakes or tornadoes ripping through cities… mostly generated by AI. At the moment, the quality is such that if you look closely enough, or perhaps are more sceptical, you will pick up details that prove them manufactured. Yet, read the comments on these videos and you'll see many people, alarmingly, believe them to be real. The real concern is that as technology improves and is so accessible, spotting the fakes is becoming harder… even for the very discerning.

AI can generate fake but realistic videos of people saying things they never said, and of politicians or celebrities saying something damaging. Or worse, people in powerful positions can dismiss real videos as deep fakes, and fake news, as their public relations strategy. How can we trust what anyone says or does these days?

As a result, we are becoming more sceptical of what we hear and what we see. It is getting harder to discern what and who we can trust.

Trust is at an all-time low because it's challenging to distinguish what is real and what is fabricated.

For the past 20 years, I have been teaching business owners, leaders and sales professionals how to share stories to create genuine, authentic connection, and I truly believe that with the increase of AI-generated content and the overall decline in trust in society, the craft of authentic storytelling is needed now more than ever.

Storytelling has been an effective means of communication for tens of thousands of years. You need only look at how Indigenous Australians (the oldest living culture) use stories to pass their knowledge and wisdom through the generations.

Interestingly, though, I don't think that AI is the devil. I know people who are so put off by the rise of AI-generated content that they refuse to use it, engage with it or even acknowledge its existence! But to ignore AI so outright would be a terrible and costly mistake. Not just because it's here to stay, and here to advance, but because AI is an incredible tool that offers so many opportunities in all sorts of personal and professional contexts.

When we learn to use AI wisely (for good, not evil, so to speak) and understand its advantages and limitations, we can use it to craft genuine stories faster and smarter.

That's what I want to show you in this book.

'Story intelligence' refers to your ability to use the skills of storytelling in an authentic way that connects, engages and inspires others, especially when mistrust is at an all-time high. There is no dictionary definition for story intelligence, so I created one:

Story intelligence (noun)

The ability to purposefully and skilfully use authentic storytelling to communicate with clarity and to connect, engage, and inspire.

If we use AI-generated stories that are not authentic, we run a serious risk to our reputation and a potential damage to our brand. So the trick is to not rely wholly on AI, but to use it as a creative partner to help uncover stories we can share to engage and inspire others; and to refine those stories and supercharge our productivity, creativity, communication skills and impact.

Think of storytelling as your Batman, and AI as your Robin, your reliable and eager sidekick.

Together, in this book, we will:

- analyse the power of storytelling and why it is needed now more than ever in a world of declining trust

- bust the myth that AI is cheating or unethical (not true if used correctly)

- deconstruct what makes a great story and how to spot a fake

- explain the limitations and advantages when it comes to AI and storytelling

- follow a framework to find stories, both with and without AI's help

- share AI tips and techniques that will improve and refine your storytelling capability

- increase your confidence to share stories in different situations, from business presentations to personal speeches

- demonstrate how others have used stories in their personal and professional lives.

To do this, part I of the book ('Understanding story intelligence') unpacks what storytelling is and what makes it so powerful.

We'll look at the latest research, which shows the decline of trust across the globe, and why authentic storytelling is needed now more than ever. We'll also put AI to the test when it comes to generating and creating stories so that you can understand its limitations and its benefits and spot a fake a mile off.

In part II ('Increasing your story intelligence'), we will delve into a comprehensive storytelling framework and explore the four types of stories you can share in certain situations. We'll also look at how you can find stories ... both with and without AI. Then we will put AI to work harder and smarter, using it as your creative partner, to help enhance your stories while maintaining your authentic voice.

Finally, in part III ('Sharing your stories'), we'll look at a variety of stories that people have shared in specific contexts: from presentations, to sales, coaching moments and delivering speeches; the results and feedback from the stories; and an analysis of why they worked. I hope these stories provide you with the inspiration to share your own stories and create the right impact and trust with others.

Now, before we get into things, it's important to note that the term 'AI' (artificial intelligence) is very broad and refers to the concept of machines or software mimicking human-like behaviour. Generative AI (Gen AI) is a subset of AI that focuses specifically on creating new content such as generating text, images, music and more ... and that is what I mostly refer to and use in this book. (If you are interacting with a chat function on a website it is most likely Gen AI.)

The two AI platforms I use and refer to in this book are ChatGPT and Claude. In some instances, I have included direct copy from these platforms to show you how they work and what they produce. When the copy is unaltered, I have used a different font to highlight this.

Note, this book will not, however, explain how ChatGPT works (there are so many great books already written on this including *The ChatGPT Revolution: How to simplify your work and life admin with AI* by Donna McGeorge). But rather, it will show you how to use AI as your creative partner to help increase your story intelligence.

So let's get ready to craft some authentic stories, made smarter with the help of AI.

PART I

Understanding story intelligence

Story intelligence is very similar to emotional intelligence in that it refers to your ability... in this case, to tell a great story (as opposed to how emotionally intelligent you are).

Just as some people are naturally better at tennis, singing or physical coordination, some may have more emotional intelligence, and others more story intelligence. In either case, the skills are always learnable and you can become better at them.

So, in this part we will explore what storytelling actually is and why stories are so powerful. We will also discover why authentic stories are needed now more than ever in a world of rising distrust. Plus, we'll begin to look at using AI as a creative partner, which means understanding the advantages and limitations of AI-generated stories.

What is storytelling and why is it so powerful?

1

When our daughter Alex was two years old and I was pregnant with our second child, Jess, we decided to put a swimming pool in our backyard.

I had always had a pool growing up and it had brought so much enjoyment. We would spend hours in that pool with all our friends, family and neighbours and I thought it would be amazing to provide the same experience to our girls.

Of course, we taught Alex and Jess how to swim as early as possible, and as they got older they would have friends over to swim. But the pool wasn't very big so when there were lots of people over for a swim, we had a strict 'no jumping in the pool' policy.

As opposed to just stating this rule to Alex and Jess, I reinforced the importance of it by sharing a story from when I was a little girl.

The story was about when their Aunty Ali (my younger sister) jumped into the pool on top of me and her knee collided with my front tooth and broke it in half (my tooth, not her knee). Aunty Ali got into a load of trouble from Nana for jumping into the pool.

Alex and Jess loved that story so much. I cannot tell you how many times they asked me to retell it. I think they liked the idea of their big, grown-up aunty getting in trouble from her mum (their nana).

Years later, when Alex was about 10 and her friends came over for a swim, I overheard her telling everyone that they were not allowed to jump into the pool. She then went on to relay the story about her Aunty Ali to explain why.

By this stage, I had been running my business storytelling workshops for years and I knew how powerful stories could be to connect with people and to get your message across more effectively in a way that was understood and remembered. So when I heard Alex retelling that story, it totally reinforced in me the true power of stories.

Messages are clearly articulated and understood through stories. Stories are remembered and, crucially, stories can be retold without losing the message.

This is the power of telling a great story. This is story intelligence in action.

So let's look at the science behind why stories are so powerful, specifically what happens in our brains when we hear good stories.

The power of stories

Our brains are complex, with different parts serving unique functions. The left hemisphere organises thoughts and handles logic, while the right hemisphere processes emotions and personal memories. Then, there's the 'reptile brain' driving instinctive actions and the 'mammal brain', which fosters social connections. Layered atop these is the neocortex, which is linked to the intricate limbic system. This network governs emotional bonds such as the connection between a mother and child.

Daniel Goleman, in his best-selling book *Emotional Intelligence*, explains the immense power of the emotions rooted in our evolved neocortex as:

> ... *the root from which the newer brain grew, the emotional areas are intertwined via myriad connecting circuits to all parts of the neocortex. This gives the emotional centres immense power to influence the functioning of the rest of the brain.*

When we tell stories, all areas of the brain (logical, emotional and sensory) are activated, working together to create vivid imagery and deep emotional resonance. A well-told story doesn't just convey information; it makes us feel something, be it excitement, empathy, pride or even sadness. These emotions form bonds between the storyteller and the audience, fostering a connection akin to the bonds formed by our limbic system.

In a 2014 *Harvard Business Review* article, neuro-economist Paul Zak highlights how storytelling stimulates oxytocin, often called the 'trust hormone'. Released during moments of trust or intimacy (such as hugging or even a handshake), oxytocin signals safety and builds trust. Remarkably, storytelling can trigger the same release, building a bond between the audience and the storyteller.

My workshops culminate in participants sharing a personal story related to a work message such as company values or purpose in small groups. Afterwards, I ask a simple question: 'What did you like about that?' Without fail, people comment that they feel a greater connection with each other.

Stories build a bond between the storyteller and their audience, which can fast track forming new relationships, or strengthen already existing relationships.

Paul Zak's research goes further, showing that storytelling doesn't just evoke oxytocin; it also releases cortisol during moments of tension, heightening focus. In one study, participants who watched an emotional story about a father and son produced both cortisol and oxytocin. Those with higher oxytocin levels were more likely to help a stranger afterwards. This demonstrates that stories with emotional highs and lows not only capture attention but also inspire empathy and action.

A good story allows listeners to feel secure, making them more likely to trust and believe the storyteller. Neuroscientist Uri Hasson explains this phenomenon as 'neural entrainment': when the brains of a storyteller and their listeners align.

In one study, listeners' brain activity mirrored the storyteller's, whether the story was in English or Russian. Essentially, hearing a story is like reliving it yourself, creating shared understanding and common ground. That's why when someone shares a story, it's very common, and surprising for some, when someone else gets emotional.

This supports the notion that experience is the best teacher, but a compelling story is a close second.

Our emotions drive decisions

We often strive to influence others through logic. Yet science shows that emotions, not logic, drive our decisions. Research by neuroscientist Antonio Damasio reveals that people with an impaired emotional centre in their brain struggle to make even simple decisions, despite having intact logical reasoning. This is because emotions provide the motivation to act; logic merely rationalises the choice afterwards. As Antonio says: 'We are not thinking machines that feel; rather, we are feeling machines that think'.

I often hear people push back on this concept, insisting that they are logical and never let emotions sway them. I call bullshit on that. Let me give you an example.

My husband, Steve, and I were discussing the potential downsizing of our family home and buying a new house over the next few years. I decided to have a quick look at what was on the market to show him the kind of house I would like, just to ensure we were on the same page when we started looking seriously.

I looked online and found a house that ticked all my boxes. I showed Steve, and he agreed that it ticked all his boxes, too. Then he suggested we go and look at it.

We walked into the house, and within minutes we had made the emotional decision to buy. The master bedroom was huge and it had a walk-in wardrobe and a spectacular ensuite. The study had floor-to-ceiling windows with ample light. The two other bedrooms were on a different floor with their own bathrooms, meaning for the very first time I no longer needed to share a bathroom with my daughters. (If you have ever had to share a bathroom with a teenager, you will no doubt appreciate the significance of this.) Steve was beside himself at the size of the garage in the basement and the close proximity to the golf course. Plus, the house had a rooftop entertainment area and was also brand new so it required significantly less maintenance than our current 120-year-old weatherboard.

We went home and spent a few days working through the pros and cons, as well as our financial situation. But let me tell you, we were coming up with some very logical reasons why we were about to spend significantly more money on a house than we had previously discussed.

Had we gone through the data and concluded that it wasn't a good decision, we would have changed our minds and decided not to buy. But it would have been a very reluctant choice because, emotionally, we were already invested. We were imagining walking to the golf course and not having to pack clubs and buggies into the car. Steve's ongoing to-do house maintenance list was disappearing before his eyes. We were imagining and getting very excited about this next stage of our lives, and a bathroom all to ourselves.

The reason we were swayed by emotion is not because we are illogical...it is because we are human. If we had gone through our financials and reached the conclusion that it would be irresponsible to buy the house but bought it anyway, that would not have been logical.

Anyone in sales or marketing will tell you that people buy on emotion and justify on logic. As Dale Carnegie, the bestselling author of *How to Win Friends and Influence People*, aptly stated, 'When dealing with people, let us remember we are not dealing with creatures of logic. We are dealing with creatures of emotion'.

Why stories stick

You probably know a family member who had a story for everything. My dad was a bit like that. In most of his teaching moments, he would tell us a story to help us understand the why and the importance of learning; for example, how to change a car tyre.

So what makes us tell a story over and over again?

Dan and Chip Heath ran an experiment that they shared in their book *Made to Stick*. It's one of my favourite business books so I have read it several times.

The experiment was conducted with students at Stanford University. Half the students were asked to prepare a one-minute speech that supported the argument that non-violent crime is a serious problem. The other half were asked to present the case against.

On average, students used two-and-a-half statistics in their one-minute speeches, while only one in ten students told a story.

When it came to remembering the presentations 10 minutes later, only 5 per cent of the audience could recall any statistics, while 63 per cent could remember the stories. If my maths serves me correctly, the stories in this experiment were around 13 times more memorable than the statistics.

I experienced this myself when I was in New York for work and took Jess along with me. We did a one-hour tour of the 9/11 Memorial Museum during which we were told lots of interesting statistics and facts. We were also told some stories of individual heroics and tragedy.

Shortly after the tour, Jess asked me if I remembered how long the guide said a particular column was. I had no idea. In fact, I could not recall one statistic, and this was only about 15 minutes after the tour had finished. The stories, however, I will remember forever.

While the facts were interesting at the time, they were not sticky. Stories, on the other hand, are sticky.

Emotion, not logic, cements memories. Whether the emotion comes from a pleasant or unpleasant story, these emotions enhance memory retention a lot better than neutral experiences, such as logical messages (for example stats and figures).

Too often, we focus solely on the importance of the message, assuming it will naturally resonate. However, without an emotional connection, even the most critical information risks being ignored or forgotten. A compelling story bridges this gap, making messages not only meaningful but memorable. Remember the pool story.

Regardless, if you are leading a change in your organisation, trying to land your dream role in a job interview, pitching to a client, giving a speech, connecting with followers on social media, teaching your students or providing a life lesson to your kids, stories will help you do this. Stories engage our brains on multiple levels, stimulate emotion and enhance memory.

If you want your audience to remember your message, then tell a story. It's how we connect, engage and inspire.

Lessons from Aristotle

In the professional world in particular, we rely heavily on using logic, and logic alone, to persuade. While facts are undeniably important, they *inform rather than influence*. We rely too heavily on spreadsheets, charts, case studies, data analysis, return on investment calculations, and so on. What we need to realise is 'Facts tell. Stories sell'.

So, to get the recipe for success right, we need to look at Aristotle's Model of Persuasion (from 350 BCE), a foundational concept in rhetoric and communication that has stood the test of time. This model, comprising ethos, pathos and logos, offers a comprehensive understanding of how individuals effectively persuade and connect with others. Each element serves a unique purpose in fostering trust and enhancing communication, making this framework particularly relevant in our personal and professional lives today.

Aristotle identified three core elements of influence:

1. *Ethos* (personal credibility)

2. *Pathos* (emotional connection)

3. *Logos* (sound logic).

Ethos (personal credibility)

Ethos refers to the credibility and ethical appeal of the speaker. It embodies the character, reliability and authority of the individual communicating a message. In both personal and professional contexts, establishing ethos is paramount for gaining trust.

For instance, in personal relationships, a friend who has consistently demonstrated honesty and support is likely to be trusted more than someone who has a history of deceit. In professional environments, ethos can manifest through expertise, experience and integrity. For example, a manager who has a proven track record of successful projects and fair treatment of employees is more likely to inspire loyalty and respect from their team. On the contrary, a leader who lacks transparency or has a history of unethical behaviour may struggle to earn the trust of their employees, leading to a toxic workplace culture.

Personal credibility is earned through authenticity, expertise and consistent alignment between words and actions. Without these, even the most logically sound arguments can fall flat.

To cultivate ethos, individuals must consistently align their actions with their words. This requires self-awareness, accountability and a commitment to ethical behaviour. Additionally, sharing personal stories or testimonials can enhance one's credibility, allowing others to see the genuine character behind the words spoken.

Pathos (emotional connection)

Pathos measures how deeply your audience engages with you and your message. It is about understanding and appealing to your audience's values, fears and aspirations.

In personal communication, pathos plays a crucial role in building empathy and understanding. For example, sharing personal struggles or successes can create a bond between friends or family members, fostering a sense of support and solidarity.

In professional contexts, pathos can be a powerful tool for leaders and marketers alike. A compelling story that resonates with employees or customers can inspire action and loyalty. For instance, a company that shares stories of how its products have positively impacted customers' lives can evoke emotional responses that enhance brand loyalty. In contrast, a purely factual presentation that lacks emotional engagement may fail to resonate with the audience, diminishing its impact.

As we have explored, stories are one of the most effective ways to build an emotional connection with your audience, especially stories that involve some level of vulnerability. However, it is essential to strike a balance because overusing emotional appeals can lead to a feeling of manipulation, which may ultimately erode trust.

Whether you're inspiring employees or a friend to embrace change, or convincing clients to choose your services, emotional connection is crucial.

Logos (sound logic)

Logos represents the logical aspect of persuasion, relying on reasoning and evidence to support claims. Using sound logic to persuade people is critical in both personal and professional communication as it provides the rational foundation for arguments and decisions.

However, while logos provides the rational foundation for decision making, it's important to understand its limitations because it is quite ineffective when it comes to persuasion or influence. Raw data and logical arguments, while necessary, rarely drive a significant change or inspire action on their own. They provide the 'what' and 'how' but often fail to address the 'why' that motivates human behaviour.

Logos alone is insufficient to inspire change.

Finding the right balance

Aristotle's model illustrates that trust is built through a combination of credibility (ethos), emotional connection (pathos) and logical reasoning (logos).

In personal relationships, these elements create a holistic approach to communication that fosters understanding and strengthens bonds. When individuals feel they can trust someone's character, relate to their emotions and understand their reasoning, they are more likely to engage openly and honestly.

Think of it like a three-legged stool. Currently, most of the way we communicate resembles a stool with one long leg (logic) and two stunted ones (credibility and emotion).

We are very, *very* good at the logic part. However, true influence emerges when logic, personal credibility and emotional connection work in harmony. So, we need to even up those leg stools. Sharing authentic stories is an extremely effective way to build personal credibility and emotional connection.

All the research shows us that stories help us to not only connect and engage but also to build trust. This has always been critical, and even more so in a world of AI, fake news and declining trust, so let's explore that next.

That's a wrap

- *Stories make meaning stick.* A simple family anecdote about a broken tooth became a memorable way to enforce pool safety, showing how stories embed lessons in a way that facts alone never could.

- *Our brains are wired for stories.* Storytelling activates multiple parts of the brain making it easier for listeners to understand, relate to and retain messages.

- *Emotion drives decision making.* Despite our belief in logic, science shows we make choices emotionally and justify them with logic afterwards. A compelling story taps into this natural process.

- *Stories create connection and trust.* When communicated authentically, stories build emotional bonds through shared experiences, triggering chemicals like oxytocin (trust) and cortisol (focus).

- *Data may inform, but stories influence.* People rarely remember stats but they remember stories. Experiments and personal experience prove stories are more memorable and impactful than pure information.

- *Aristotle's timeless model of ethos (credibility), pathos (emotion) and logos (logic) reminds us that persuasion is a balance of all three.* Stories offer a way to build trust and connection alongside rational arguments.

Why stories are so crucial today

2

Remember the Information Age in the 1990s after the internet burst into our lives? That feeling of information overload pales into insignificance with AI. We not only have more information at our fingertips, we also have to determine whether it's fake or real. Whether it's intended with good intent or manipulation. We have moved from the Information Age to the Trust Age, or perhaps more accurately, the Distrust Age.

Misinformation often feels like it is weaponised, not just to deceive but to divide. And through it all, the very idea of 'what is truth' comes under pressure.

This is why authentic storytelling is so crucial today...because we are in a trust crisis.

The Edelman Trust Barometer has been providing a comprehensive analysis of global trust across key institutions (business, government, non-governmental organisations (NGOs) and media) for over 25 years. I have been following the annual publication for years and it's interesting to note where we are currently at.

The 2025 report surveyed over 33 000 people from 28 countries and their key findings on the global decline of trust is disturbing.

Some of the key findings showed that the majority of respondents hold grievances against government, business and the rich. Sixty-one per cent globally have a moderate or high sense of grievance, which is defined by a belief that government and business make their lives harder and serve narrow interests, and wealthy people benefit unfairly from the system while regular people struggle.

The report also found that this widespread grievance erodes trust and that those with a high sense of grievance do not trust any of the four institutions (business, government, media and NGOs). Additionally, they do not trust CEOs or AI.

Here's what's alarming:

- *Global trust has stagnated at 56 per cent globally.* Trust levels vary significantly by country, with China, Indonesia and India reporting the highest levels of trust; and Japan, the UK and Germany reporting the lowest. Trust inequality between high-income and low-income groups has widened, with low-income individuals showing significant distrust toward institutions.

- *Governments are least trusted and this is particularly high in Western democracies.* Countries that underwent elections in 2024, such as the United States, the UK and France, showed little to no improvement in trust levels. Business was the most trusted institution, though there are still concerns about ethical responsibilities.

- *For the first time ever, trust in employers has dropped globally.* The report signalled concerns about job security, automation and corporate ethics, something all leaders should be mindful of when it comes to communication.

- *The role of misinformation and AI is high.* Fear of purposely misleading the people by saying things they know are false or grossly exaggerated has reached an all-time high. In summary, 69 per cent are concerned about government leaders misleading people, 68 per cent are concerned with business leaders and 70 per cent are concerned about journalists and reporters misleading people. I find this extraordinarily high. When you flip the numbers, that means only 30 per cent of people are not concerned about being misled.

The report indicates that institutional failures over the past 25 years have led to a widespread crisis of grievance. This makes it critical for leaders, especially in business, to take active steps to rebuild trust through ethical leadership, transparency and meaningful societal engagement.

The World Economic Forum's Global Risks Report 2025 also backs up these findings. The report highlights a significant decline in trust, particularly concerning AI and the proliferation of disinformation.

Key findings of the report include:

- *Misinformation and disinformation are the top risks for the second consecutive year.* These factors erode societal cohesion and undermine trust in governance, complicating efforts to address shared crises.

- *AI's amplification of false information.* The report emphasises what we already know: the advancements in AI have significantly lowered the barriers to producing and distributing false or misleading content. This technology enables the rapid creation and spread of deepfakes, synthetic voice recordings and fabricated news stories, making it increasingly challenging to distinguish between genuine and deceptive information.

- *There's an erosion of trust in institutions.* The pervasive spread of AI-generated disinformation undermines public trust in critical institutions, including governments and the media. It highlights that this erosion of trust poses a substantial threat to democratic processes and societal stability.

In short, AI will continue to evolve, deepfakes will become even more convincing and misinformation will persist. The battle for trust will define the coming decades.

So what does all this mean for us?

We cannot rely on polished messaging; perfectly curated, or even AI-generated, images; or corporate-speak. People are looking for real voices, raw honesty and a sense that there are actual humans behind the brand. Even with the popularity of content creators and influencers, people are looking to connect to a real person…someone they can trust.

In a world flooded with artificially generated content, our very humanness becomes a differentiator. Individuals, professionals, and leaders must learn to show up with greater authenticity. We must share real stories with each other!

Sharing authentic stories is critical to address our key challenges:

- How do we earn trust in a time of widespread distrust?

- How do we stand out when AI can mimic our voice and our face?

- How do we rise above the noise of fake news and constant spin?

You cannot control others sharing misinformation and fake stories, but you can control the stories you choose to share with genuine intent.

In a world of distrust, your audience is highly sceptical, so the stories you share cannot afford to have any elements that 'just don't seem believable'. That means, your stories need to be true and cannot be made up by AI alone. AI cannot run the show (more on that soon).

In an age of distrust, authentic stories are your greatest asset, maybe even your superpower.

Technology is not the enemy

With that said, ignoring AI completely would be at your peril...especially when it comes to storytelling.

Sure, if you look at the previous stats, AI is contributing to the decline of trust because it is an unknown force, but it is definitely *not* the enemy. AI is arguably the greatest technical advancement of this century and it is being embraced at breakneck speed!

For example, did you know that within five days of launching in 2022, ChatGPT had one million users? To put that into context, it took Instagram five months to get a million users, Facebook 10 months and Netflix three-and-a-half years.

However, with any new technology and all the benefits it brings, there are always negative consequences. (I mean, before electricity, no-one died from being electrocuted.)

We are at the very early stages of truly understanding the benefits and consequences of AI. So, given what AI is capable of, many people understandably feel concerned about using it, whether it's 'right', 'wrong' or contributing to trust problems.

While the speed at which AI is infiltrating our lives can feel overwhelming or exciting... or both... we need to do our best to stay current. Many people are concerned they will lose their job to AI. The most likely scenario is that you will lose your job to someone who has embraced AI. Our employers will expect us to embrace this technology soon enough, if they haven't already.

And when used correctly and with integrity, AI is absolutely amazing! On a global scale, it is touted to transform healthcare from finding cures for cancer to providing more accurate and faster diagnoses. On a personal level, AI cannot only save you time and energy but it can also significantly help with your creativity, especially when it comes to generating and refining your stories. (I will prove that to you soon.)

When ChatGPT came along I started to experiment and use it to edit my LinkedIn posts, and to reword emails to make them sound more professional and succinct, or less defensive. I also started to use it for other things, such as idea generation for articles.

Given the nature of my work, I also started to experiment with using AI to generate stories.

I would use AI to suggest stories to me about a specific topic. For example, teamwork or innovation. To my surprise, what AI generated wasn't that bad. In most instances, they were plausible stories and definitely something I could work with. But never something I would just straight out share! So my whole premise for this book is to help you adopt this amazing technology to help increase your storytelling intelligence.

Now, I am by no means an expert on AI... far from it. But I do enjoy keeping up with emerging technology and am a bit obsessed with efficiency (probably because I am inherently impatient).

You don't need to understand how things like AI work to make them work *for* you. (For example, I have no freaking idea how a microwave works, but it has not stopped me from using it for most of my life.)

So, in the next chapter we're going to put this technology to the test. Let's look at the limitations and advantages of using AI to help you with your stories. We'll learn to spot a fake, and make sure you're not creating your own fakes and adding to the mistrust out there.

When you know how to tell a great story, and how to use AI to help, your storytelling intelligence knows no bounds.

That's a wrap

- *We've entered the Distrust Age.* From the optimism of the Information Age, we've now arrived at a time where trust is under siege. Misinformation is weaponised, and the line between truth and manipulation is increasingly blurred.

- *Global trust is in freefall.* The 2025 Edelman Trust Barometer and the World Economic Forum's Global Risks Report show alarming trends: trust in institutions, leaders, media and AI is eroding, especially in Western democracies. Trust in employers has dropped for the first time ever.

- *People crave realness, not perfection.* Polished messaging and corporate-speak no longer cut through. In a world of deepfakes and content overload, we are hungry for raw honesty, emotional truth and genuine connection.

- *Authentic storytelling is your trust-building superpower.* In an age of AI-generated content and digital noise, sharing personal, human stories is one of the most powerful ways to stand out, earn trust, connect and inspire others.

- *You can't control misinformation, but you can control your own stories.* People are sceptical, so your stories must be real. They can't feel 'off' or manufactured. True, lived experiences build credibility and that's something AI alone can't fake.

- *AI isn't the enemy... but it's not the answer either.* Like electricity, AI is powerful but must be used wisely. It can assist with efficiency, creativity and editing but it can't replace your lived experiences or emotional truth.

Putting AI to the test... the pros and cons

3

Humans have had a long obsession with pitting themselves against computers, and one of the most well-known of these was with chess.

In May 1997, IBM's Deep Blue computer and world-class chess champion Garry Kasparov played a six-game match in New York City under standard chess tournament conditions.

Kasparov, who was then the world's top-ranked chess player, had first played Deep Blue in 1996, winning the match 4–2. Over the subsequent months, the IBM programmers continually taught the machine to evaluate more chess positions and calculate potential moves with unprecedented speed. According to the IBM website, Deep Blue was capable of calculating 200 million chess positions per second.

The 1997 rematch saw Deep Blue win the match 3.5–2.5. It was the first time a computer had defeated a world champion in a match. In the second game, Deep Blue made a stunning and totally unexpected move. It sacrificed a pawn in a way that demonstrated insights previously thought to be beyond the capability of a machine.

It is reported that Kasparov was visibly shaken, interpreting the move as evidence of human-like intuition. He later said, 'For the first time in the history of mankind, I saw something similar to an artificial intellect', describing the experience as deeply unsettling.

In a bit of a no-shit Sherlock moment, Kasparov felt that the computer's ability to calculate millions of potential moves in seconds fundamentally changed the nature of chess strategy.

The match sparked global discussions about the future of AI, human intelligence and the potential of machines to compete with and potentially surpass human capabilities in intellectual pursuits.

It was perhaps our first glimpse of the incredible potential of artificial intelligence and the complex human emotions surrounding such technological advancements.

IBM's C J Tan, who is now retired but led the development of Deep Blue, reflected on the result: 'Garry prepared to play against a computer. But we programmed it to play like a grandmaster'.

This contest proved that computers can be better than humans at some things, like chess. And it got me thinking, how would AI stack up in a contest against authentic storytelling, AE (Authentic Experience), as it were? What if there was a match between me (from the AE corner) against AI: my story intelligence pitched against the best that AI can come up with?

I put AI to the storytelling test so we can learn the pros and cons of using it and identify what we need to watch out for; to help you spot a fake AI generated story and to encourage you to always share genuine and real stories.

The storytelling contest

For the contest, I pitched my human storytelling skills against the storytelling abilities of ChatGPT and Claude. I followed the standard chess tournament approach and decided on six rounds. I then chose six different topics that we would all share stories about, such as stories about the dangers of making assumptions or stories about empowering your teams.

Using specific prompts, I asked ChatGPT and Claude to share a story from the first-person perspective for each topic. I then documented my own story for each.

This resulted in a total of 18 stories: three for each topic (mine, ChatGPT's and Claude's).

I then asked some people to rate each story. They had no indication of which story was generated from which source. Very much like a blind taste test. They also had *no idea that any of the stories were generated from AI.* I simply asked people to rate them.

Now, in total transparency, the sample size was only 21 people, so most likely this test would not stand up to any academic rigour. But I did this research out of curiosity, to test my hypothesis around AI and storytelling.

Each participant was asked to rate each story on five elements:

1. *Clarity:* The story is clear and logical.

2. *Engagement:* The story held my attention the whole way through.

3. *Emotional impact:* I feel connected to the storyteller and their personal experience.

4. *Authenticity:* The story feels real and authentic.

5. *Memorability:* The message of the story is easy to remember.

Before I reveal the results, let's dissect three of the 18 stories together, to give you an opportunity to rate them and test this process for yourself.

The following three stories are related to having the courage to back yourself. As you read each story, rate each one out of 5, based on the above criteria. For example, a rating of 1 or 2 for Clarity would indicate that the story is not very clear or logical, while a rating of 4 or 5 would indicate the story is very clear and logical.

Let's begin!

Story 1

For most of my life, I was the person who stayed in the shadows. Not because I didn't have anything to offer, but because I was terrified of what might happen if I stepped into the spotlight. What if I failed? Worse, what if everyone saw me fail? So, I played it safe at work, in relationships, in pretty much everything. Until the day I didn't.

It all started with a meeting at work. My boss was assigning the lead role for a new project, a major one that could fast track someone's career. The room was quiet, the kind of quiet that settles in when everyone's too afraid to volunteer but secretly hopes to be picked. I was sitting there, heart pounding, my inner voice screaming, You could do this. You should do this.

But then the doubts crept in. What if you mess it up? What if you're not good enough? I stared at the table, trying to shrink into invisibility. But then my boss said something that changed everything: 'This is a great opportunity, but it's only for someone willing to take a risk'.

I looked around the room. No-one moved. And then, almost involuntarily, I raised my hand. 'I'll do it,' I said, my voice a little shakier than I'd hoped.

Everyone turned to look at me. My boss raised an eyebrow, clearly surprised. 'You sure?' he asked.

'Yes,' I said, louder this time. And just like that, I was in.

Walking out of that meeting, I was exhilarated and terrified. I had no idea if I could pull it off, but for the first time, I didn't care. I was tired of waiting for someone else to validate me, tired of holding back out of fear. If I failed, I told myself, at least I'd fail knowing I had tried.

The weeks that followed were some of the hardest of my life. I had to make decisions I wasn't sure about, present ideas to senior executives and, worst of all, trust that I was capable. There were moments when I questioned myself, but every time, I reminded myself why I'd raised my hand in the first place: because I believed, deep down, that I could do it.

And I did. The project was a success. Better than anyone had expected. But the real victory wasn't the outcome; it was the process. For the first time, I backed myself, and it worked.

That moment taught me something I'll carry forever: courage isn't about being fearless. It's about raising your hand even when you're scared. It's about betting on yourself, even when you're not sure how it will turn out. And sometimes, that's all it takes to change everything.

How would you rate story 1 according to the five criteria: Clarity, Engagement, Emotional impact, Authenticity and Memorability?

Turn to table 3.1 on page 31 to record your answers.

Story 2

The application sat on my desk for weeks, the edges growing slightly dog-eared from my nervous handling. A fellowship to study marine conservation in the Galápagos, something I'd dreamed about since I was a kid watching nature documentaries in our small apartment. But every time I looked at it, a chorus of doubting voices crowded my mind.

'You're not good enough,' whispered the voice that sounded suspiciously like my high school guidance counsellor, who'd once told me research wasn't for "people like me". My parents, immigrants who had worked multiple jobs to give me opportunities, would worry about the financial uncertainty. My colleagues at the marine biology lab seemed to have more published papers, more connections, more of everything.

The deadline was three days away, and I hadn't submitted a single document.

It was my grandmother who changed everything. She'd survived a civil war, travelled across an ocean with nothing but a suitcase and hope, and built a life from scratch.

When I explained my hesitations, she looked at me with those eyes that had seen real challenges and said, 'Mija, the only person stopping you is yourself'.

That night, I rewrote my personal statement with a fury I didn't know I possessed. I poured every passionate observation from my years of marine research into those pages. The countless hours I'd spent cataloguing microplastic pollution in local waterways. The community education programs I'd developed. The innovative sampling techniques I'd refined.

When I finally submitted the application, I felt something shift inside me. It wasn't about whether I would get the fellowship. It was about proving to myself that I was worthy of my own dreams.

Two months later, the email arrived. Not just an acceptance, but a full fellowship with additional funding for my specific research proposal. The selection committee was particularly impressed by my community-focused approach to marine conservation.

What struck me most wasn't the achievement itself, but the realisation that my self-doubt had almost prevented me from even trying. How many opportunities do we miss by listening to those internal critics? How many dreams remain unlived because we're too afraid to back ourselves?

My grandmother was right. The only real limitation is the one we place on ourselves. Backing yourself isn't about guaranteeing success; it's about giving yourself the chance to succeed. It's about understanding that your worth isn't determined by external validation, but by the courage to step into the arena, regardless of the outcome.

How would you rate story 2 according to the five criteria: Clarity, Engagement, Emotional impact, Authenticity and Memorability?

Turn to table 3.1 on page 31 to record your answers.

Story 3

In my mid twenties I joined a softball club. I played for a short time at school and wanted to take up the sport again.

Being a non-professional club, all players were expected to regularly undertake umpiring duties. You would start by being a line umpire, while the more experienced players would undertake the main umpiring duties. These are the umpires that crouch right behind the catcher calling strikes, balls and 'You're out'.

After a couple of years, I was 'voluntold' by the president of the club to umpire a match as the main umpire. While I was capable enough, it was still very daunting.

Just before the match, I was speaking to the president, who was also a teammate. Hence, she knew me well. I suggested to her that before the match I would tell both sides that this was my first match I have ever umpired as the main umpire. So, I might make mistakes but go easy on me.

I still remember her looking me in the eye and saying, 'No you won't say that. You will go out there and make the calls confidently, like you have done this many times before. No-one needs to know this is your first time'.

She followed this up with, 'I would not have asked you to umpire if I didn't have full confidence in your capability to do so. You've got this'.

And you know what?

I did have it. I called every ball, strike and out, with more and more confidence each time.

The positive offshoot was that my confidence also filled the players and their supporters with the confidence that I had made the correct calls. No arguments, no descent and no feeling they had been short-changed with an inexperienced umpire.

I am sharing this with you because often in business our own lack of confidence can have a negative impact on the people around us.

You see this often when people get a promotion.

No-one gives you a promotion if they don't think you can do the job … no-one. They are a better judge of your capability than you.

So, forget the crap of 'fake it until you make it' or 'fake it until you feel it'.

You are not faking anything.

You have the capability. Your confidence may just take a little while to catch up.

So, when you are next feeling a lack of confidence, acknowledge it and look in the mirror and say, 'You've got this'.

Because you no doubt have.

How would you rate story 3 according to the five criteria: Clarity, Engagement, Emotional impact, Authenticity and Memorability?

Fill in your ratings for story 3 in table 3.1.

Rate each story between 1 to 5 (with 1 being low, and 5 being high) for each of the five criteria.

Table 3.1   the storytelling ratings

Criteria	Story 1	Story 2	Story 3
Clarity: The story is clear and logical			
Engagement: The story held my attention the whole way through			
Emotional impact: I feel connected to the storyteller and their personal experience			
Authenticity: The story feels real and authentic			
Memorability: The message of the story is easy to remember			
Total			

Which story did you rate the highest?

The results

Before I reveal the author of each of the above stories, let's look at the results in table 3.2 from the 21 participants who rated the stories.

Table 3.2 ratings from the three featured stories

Story 1	Rating
Clarity: The story is clear and logical	4.4
Engagement: The story held my attention the whole way through	4.2
Emotional impact: I feel connected to the storyteller and their personal experience	4.3
Authenticity: The story feels real and authentic	4.1
Memorability: The message of the story is easy to remember	4.4
Overall average rating	**4.3**
Story 2	**Rating**
Clarity: The story is clear and logical	4.2
Engagement: The story held my attention the whole way through	4.0
Emotional impact: I feel connected to the storyteller and their personal experience	4.0
Authenticity: The story feels real and authentic	3.9
Memorability: The message of the story is easy to remember	4.1
Overall average rating	**4.0**
Story 3	**Rating**
Clarity: The story is clear and logical	4.5
Engagement: The story held my attention the whole way through	4.5

Story 3	Rating
Emotional impact: I feel connected to the storyteller and their personal experience	4.5
Authenticity: The story feels real and authentic	4.6
Memorability: The message of the story is easy to remember	4.7
Overall average rating	**4.6**

So, overall story 3 was the winner.

But whose story was it?

Story 1 was ChatGPT. Story 2 was Claude and story 3 was mine.

I have only shown the ratings of the three stories above, but it's best to look at the average ratings for all 18 stories to get an indication of where AI performed better.

Each story was rated from 1 to 5 against each of the five criteria to get an average score for each one. In table 3.3, I have listed the average for each criterion and ChatGPT's and Claude's combined averages to get an average AI score. I then compared the average combined AI score to my score to find the difference.

Table 3.3 ratings from the 18 tested stories

Criteria	ChatGPT	Claude	AI combined average	Me	Difference
Clarity	4.15	4.08	4.11	4.29	+ 0.18
Engagement	3.92	3.80	3.86	4.28	+ 0.42
Emotional impact	3.98	3.83	3.90	4.17	+ 0.27
Authenticity	3.90	3.76	3.83	4.28	+ 0.45
Memorability	4.14	3.95	4.04	4.33	+ 0.29
Overall rating	**4.01**	**3.88**	**3.94**	**4.27**	**+ 0.33**

Where AI did okay

Overall, the results proved that AI-generated stories are okay … and sometimes pretty good. Out of the six groups of stories, my stories were rated higher than ChatGPT's and Claude's four out of six times. So, it wasn't a clean-sweep win for me. In one instance, ChatGPT's story was rated higher than mine, and in another instance, it was a three-way draw.

Even though I won four of the six matches, in some instances my human story was only rated slightly higher than my AI opponents'. So AI performed well and I must admit it performed above my expectations.

When you look at the average rating of all 18 stories in table 3.3, AI rated quite well with regard to Clarity, with just a slightly lower than what my stories rated for Clarity.

AI also rated okay for Memorability and Emotional impact. Like my story, both of the AI stories included elements of vulnerability by questioning their own self-doubt and lack of confidence. This certainly helped them rate well on Emotional impact and Memorability.

What AI lacked

The AI stories rated much lower than my stories for Engagement. The biggest gap between the AI stories and mine was for Authenticity.

So while the AI stories' highest average rating was Clarity, their lowest average rating was Authenticity.

Let's go back to the three featured stories for a moment and specifically look at the rating of Clarity compared to Authenticity. For my story, Clarity was rated at 4.5 and Authenticity was rated higher at 4.6. However, Claude's story was rated at 4.2 for Clarity while it was rated significantly lower at 3.9 for Authenticity. The same with ChatGPT's story: Clarity was rated at 4.4 but Authenticity was rated at only 4.1.

Sometimes it's hard to really put your finger on why a story feels inauthentic. So let's look at the two AI-generated stories more closely along with some of the tell-tale signs that negatively impacted their believability.

Story 1

In story 1 the language was too flowery: 'The room was quiet, the kind of quiet that settles in when everyone's too afraid to volunteer but secretly hopes to be picked. I was sitting there, heart pounding, my inner voice screaming, "You could do this. You should do this".'

What's more, 'secretly hopes to be picked' seems inaccurate here. If you're a person who is 'terrified' of the spotlight, then it makes more sense that you are secretly hoping you are *not* picked.

It also sounds cliché in that the writer had spent their whole life in the shadows and was 'terrified' to step into the spotlight, and then in one moment volunteered for something big that magically changed everything. I'm not buying it.

Story 2

Story 2 also had overly flowery phrases like 'edges growing slightly dog-eared from my nervous handling'. It also came across as cliché. Really doubting herself and then one bit of advice completely transforms her? Not likely.

And did you find this sentence hard to believe: 'Two months later, the email arrived. Not just an acceptance, but a full fellowship with additional funding for my specific research proposal'?

Surely, there would have been interviews conducted to be accepted with a full fellowship and additional funding. Again, I'm not buying it.

This lack of feeling authentic is a significant finding as it highlights the limitation of using AI-generated stories alone. On the surface, the stories can look like a good story. They have clarity, they follow a logical structure and the message is clear … but they don't feel real or authentic.

My stories were very different: on average, they were rated almost the same on Clarity (4.29) and Authenticity (4.28), meaning when people read my stories there wasn't a disconnect between the story being clear and the story feeling real and authentic.

Among the AI-generated stories there was a much bigger gap. All 12 of the AI-generated stories rated lower on Authenticity than Clarity. So, although the stories were clear, they lacked authenticity.

It wasn't only the qualitative data that showed this; the quantitative data revealed the same findings.

In conversations with some of the respondents afterwards, I found that their feedback shone a light on the limitations of the AI-generated stories.

A few of the participants told me that when rating the stories they were trying to be nice but they felt some of them were simply cringeworthy, making them switch off. Unbeknown to the participants, they were, of course, the AI-generated ones.

My strong belief about why these stories evoked a cringe response is because they are cliché. The more generic and cliché your stories are, the less people will connect with them.

One person I asked (Arthur) did not complete the test and therefore is not part of the official sample size. For context, the first two stories in the test were AI generated. Arthur sent me a text:

I've got to be honest, Gabrielle, I read and rated the first two stories but I didn't get motivated to tackle the next 16. The stories don't quite feel 'real' or 'authentic' to me by the wording. Sorry.

No sorry at all required, Arthur, because that is exactly what AI-generated stories feel like … not real or authentic. Because they are not.

★ ★ ★ ★ ★

The contest proved my starting hypothesis, which was that AI-generated stories are good, but they lack something. The contest showed that what they lacked was engagement and authenticity … they just didn't feel believable.

AI-generated stories definitely have their limitations and I would never suggest you use an AI-generated story and share it as if it was yours. But there are lots of benefits to using AI as your creative partner, the Robin to your Batman. Let's look at why in the next chapter.

That's a wrap

- *AI can mimic structure, but not lived experience.* A 'storytelling match' between my stories and two AI models (ChatGPT and Claude) revealed a key insight: AI stories are clear and logical, but often lack emotional depth and believability.

- *The blind test results were revealing.* Across 18 stories rated by participants, my stories consistently scored higher on Authenticity and Engagement. AI stories were rated well for Clarity, but felt less real. There was a noticeable gap between how logical and how genuine they appeared.

- *Clichés and over-polish are red flags.* Participants described some AI-generated stories as 'cringe-worthy'. Flowery language, convenient plot twists and overly idealistic outcomes often made them feel fabricated.

- *Emotional truth can't be automated.* Even well-written stories that follow a solid narrative arc fall short if they don't reflect a personal, lived experience. Authenticity and vulnerability are hard for AI to replicate convincingly.

- *Your audience can tell the difference.* Readers may not know exactly why something feels 'off', but they can sense when a story lacks authenticity. That gut feeling is your audience's trust radar…and in storytelling, that's *everything*!

Embracing AI as your creative partner

4

Imagine you walk into a library and there are two librarians on duty. You approach the first librarian, called Google, and ask if you can have some information on how to build your own self-watering garden bed. This very useful librarian knows where all the books and articles are on this subject and points you in that direction. You can then start to read all the articles and books and take notes. Some may be useful, some may not be.

There is also a new librarian on duty who you haven't seen before called AI. So you ask AI the same question. The difference with this new librarian, however, is that they have read every single article and book in the library and have the most amazing photographic memory. So, instead of pointing you in the right direction, they summarise all that they have read and produce a succinct report for you.

They then ask if you would like more information on a specific aspect of the report. They might even ask if you would like a diagram or image of the garden bed and some advice on what to plant in the garden bed. They would most certainly suggest the problems you should look out for when building a self-watering garden bed and what you could do to minimise these problems.

Now, I don't know about you, and I certainly don't want to disparage the old librarian called Google because they have been very useful over the past few decades, but the next time I go to the library, I'm making a beeline for AI.

Just as Google could send you to a reference that may or may not be useful, or in fact true, the same will happen with AI. You see AI is new to being a librarian and they are very eager to please. So sometimes they can make stuff up in their eagerness to please you. This is called hallucinating... and in fairness we have all been guilty of that.

So it is critical when using AI as your creative partner that you always check for accuracy. (We'll learn to do that in subsequent chapters.) This is your responsibility as the storyteller. Increasing your story intelligence heightens your innate sense of whether a story feels real. This results in increasing your chances of more effectively connecting, engaging and inspiring.

But first, let's address something that's likely in the back of your mind... a potential elephant in the room.

Is using AI cheating?

There may be no elephant in your room, but I have met many people who feel that using AI is cheating and, in principle, refuse to use it. Specifically, I have heard many journalists and writers say this. It feels a bit like refusing to use a calculator because it's cheating.

I understand the principle behind why some people feel this, and often think it comes from a sense of nostalgia. Because sometimes you can get real pleasure and pride from doing things by hand: like baking a cake from scratch instead of using a packet mix, or using sticks to start a fire.

We have a holiday property that is 25 acres of bush land and when the sun drops, we often sit around the campfire. To get the fire started we need to first collect dried leaves, kindling and fallen branches. On our property, we have several types of gum tree, including stringy bark gum. Due to its highly flammable properties, the bark of a stringy bark serves as a natural firelighter. So at all times, I try to avoid using paper and store-bought firelighters to start the fire as I feel a sense of accomplishment and nostalgia when I can start a fire from scratch.

Having said that, I do use a gas firelighter or matches as I haven't quite mastered the art of starting a fire with sticks. But most of the time I find that I can get the fire started with dried leaves and stringy bark. It does take longer but I feel a greater satisfaction for doing it myself without interventions.

In some cases, when we have had lots of rain, it is very hard to find dry leaves and kindling and we have to resort to using paper and firelighters to get the fire started.

Is that cheating? I don't think so. It's using the available resources to get the fire started ... to create that spark.

I see AI in the same vein: using available resources to create that spark. In this case, your creative spark.

It could feel more nostalgic not to use AI in writing, perhaps the same way as it could feel nostalgic to use an old-fashioned typewriter instead of a laptop, but it's not very efficient.

You will, of course, make your own decision on when and where to use AI. But I don't see it as cheating.

For example, I used AI to help in the creative process of this book. For every step of writing any book, I involved other people and their contributions. Whether it's feedback on early drafts, editing or deciding on a book title and subtitle, they all play a part in shaping the final product. And yet, I don't think anyone would call that 'cheating'. On the contrary, most people would say it's smart to seek input from experts and collaborators.

This is the eighth book I've published, but it's the first time I've used AI as part of the process. So am I cheating by using AI to help with the written word or process?

To answer that question, let me break down the process I undertake when writing a book:

- *Writing content.* I start by writing LinkedIn posts and, based on the engagement and feedback from those pieces, I ask myself, 'Could this be a book?'

- *Brainstorming concepts.* I map out the potential main concepts for the book, usually alone, and then meet with my publisher to seek feedback and refine the direction.

- *Refining the outline.* Using this feedback, I draft and redraft the overall structure, often involving input from others. I might even post on LinkedIn to ask my audience what they'd like to see included in the book.

- *Completing an author proposal for the publisher.* I need to submit a proposal about the aim of the book, audience, marketing plan, potential competitors, my bio, and how I will promote and sell the book.

- *Writing the manuscript.* Once the framework feels solid, I dive into the writing process.

- *Editing and reworking.* The manuscript then goes through several layers of editing, both my initial editing as I write and then working with my own professional editor. These steps usually involve rewrites after rewrites.

- *Publisher review.* After submitting my manuscript to the publisher, there's another round of edits, with more rewriting... hopefully minimal by this stage.

- *Final touches.* I and a professional proofreader then proofread the manuscript before it's finally ready to go.

That's just the writing process, but it's worth mentioning that publishing involves many other tasks, such as crafting titles and subtitles, designing covers and marketing the book.

So, how does AI fit in?

AI is a tool, much like my publisher's conceptual feedback and the professional editor's insights into structure and content. AI doesn't write the book for me; it assists me, making parts of the process faster or more efficient.

For example, AI can help generate ideas for titles and subtitles. It has been my experience that coming up with the title and subtitle of a book can be a frustrating experience, mainly because so many people need to agree on it.

So this time I decided to use AI to come up with suggestions. I was very specific with the prompt I used, explaining to ChatGPT that it was predominantly a storytelling book but using AI as a tool to help with personal and professional stories.

One of the titles AI suggested was 'Narrative Intelligence'. I'm not a fan of the word 'narrative', mainly because I see people overuse the word and incorrectly interchange it with the word 'story'. But I really like the word 'intelligence', so I replaced 'narrative' with 'story' and *voilà! Story Intelligence* became the book's title. It also made me think of emotional intelligence, which I felt was an appropriate link to storytelling.

I doubt I would have come up with this title without the input of AI. What I have no doubt about is how efficient the process was this time around.

Next, you need a subtitle. This is always tricky because it has to capture what the book is about using very few words. I started with some subtitles and then turned to ChatGPT for suggestions. I chose the ones I preferred from ChatGPT, altering some, and forwarded them to my publisher and editor for feedback. We eventually landed on one, but it still didn't seem right to me.

After more suggestions and conversations, I turned to my friend Kieran Flanagan. Kieran is a guru around creativity and marketing and she provided me with a heap of suggestions. Though I had a favourite, I sent Kieran's full list of subtitle suggestions to my publisher. They did an internal poll with a few of the team and their overwhelming favourite was also my choice. Finally, we had our subtitle. This provides a perfect example of how AI is just one member of your creative team...but not the most creative member.

AI can also help in suggesting engaging copy for the book's back cover blurb. It can provide design ideas and marketing strategies. It can help summarise sections of the book into shareable articles or posts.

It even helped me write my author's proposal. When completing the proposal for this book and answering the question, 'Who would be the market', I turned to the list of 50 people generated by ChatGPT who might benefit from this book. I then selected the top 10 who I thought were the most relevant and added them to my own list.

All in all, AI is just one more addition to my creative team. Using AI saves time, but it doesn't replace the creativity or decision-making processes that make the book mine.

A brilliant brainstorming tool

Regardless, whether it is writing a book, or choosing the next family travel destination, or brainstorming a challenge with your team, you should consider bringing in AI to help.

The greatest advantage of using AI as your creative partner is that its 'creativity' is limitless. It can produce more ideas more quickly than we humans.

For example, early on in the process of writing this book, I asked ChatGPT to offer me some possibilities regarding who would benefit from a book on AI and storytelling. The responses were pretty accurate and gave me some good ideas, such as content creators and teachers. Intrigued, I asked several more times.

Within a few minutes, ChatGPT had provided over 50 possibilities. The pure efficiency of this is a game changer! Even if I had five people around the table following the brainstorming process and asked the same question, it would take a lot longer than a few minutes to have answers. By the time the five people came into the room, grabbed a coffee, said their hellos and sat down, AI would have already done the job. It's like the traditional brainstorming process on steroids... significantly more ideas in a fraction of the time (plus, I can call on AI at any time of the day or night).

The other benefit is that AI did not succumb to judging the ideas until I specifically asked it to.

You, too, have most likely found yourself in a brainstorming session before, where you sit around a table generating a whole lot of ideas. Whether that's to solve a problem at work or scenario planning or product ideas... or even sitting around the family table to decide what holiday to plan next.

The one rule with brainstorming sessions is that no idea is a bad idea. The theory being that unconventional ideas can lead to better ideas. A quantity-over-quality approach is encouraged, as well as suspending any form of criticism or judgement of a particular suggestion.

But what usually happens when everyone is generating all these ideas is that someone feels the need to jump in with 'that won't work' or 'we tried that a few years ago and it failed'. This results in ideas being shut down before they are fully explored. It can also have a negative effect on people, stopping them from suggesting ideas if they feel they are going to be judged as ridiculous ideas.

When we include AI as our creative partner, however, we open our world to many brainstorming advantages that the human process does not allow.

The first is that AI does not succumb to those natural human tendencies of thinking, 'What if people ridicule my idea...maybe I won't say it'. It also does not succumb to the natural tendency of wanting to point out why things won't work. Probably because it is not human. You can simply ask AI to provide some ideas and it will. Then ask for more ideas and it will oblige.

So, I'm not suggesting you totally replace asking humans for ideas, but rather that you include AI as part of your creative team, which brings me to Elizabeth Gilbert.

The relationship I have developed with AI, especially in the context of today and all the worry and mistrust in the world, reminds me of the relationship between fear and creativity that Elizabeth Gilbert writes about in her book *Big Magic*.

Gilbert talks about fear as being part of creativity. She acknowledges it is there but doesn't let it drive her decisions. She has even penned a letter to her fear, ready to send it whenever she embarks on a creative endeavour. The main premise of her letter is that fear can come along on the ride with creativity but it is never allowed to take control of the steering wheel.

Inspired by Gilbert, I've created my own letter, not to fear but to AI.

Dearest AI,

Creativity and I are about to go on a road trip together. I invite you to join us.

I will be doing my job on this road trip, which is to work hard and stay focused. And Creativity will be doing its job, which is to remain stimulating and inspiring.

There is plenty of room in this vehicle for all of us, so make yourself at home, but understand this:

Creativity and I are the only ones who will be making any decision along the way. I recognise and respect the supporting and valuable role you can play. So I will at times ask you for advice and suggestions along the way.

But understand that I will always make the final decision and I will always be in control. Don't take this personally, as I know you won't because you are not a person. But I know sometimes, while you are eager, you hallucinate, so sometimes you are wrong. You also come with some built-in biases so we are not always aligned.

So you're allowed to have a seat, and you're allowed to have a voice when asked, but my dear friend AI, you are absolutely forbidden to drive. I will always be in control.

So if you don't let AI take control of the wheel then you can use it to your advantage. If you come from a place of authenticity, your stories have the ability to be one of your most powerful communication tools. But storytelling is a skill. Increasing your story intelligence is a commitment, one that I guarantee you will pay off in spades. Storytelling is a human trait and AI cannot replicate your own authentic stories. Don't succumb to the easy path of using AI generated stories... you are better than that. Do the work needed to tell great stories.

In part II of the book, we will explore how to do this... to increase your story intelligence to help you better connect, engage and inspire with and without AI.

That's a wrap

- *AI isn't cheating. It's collaborating.* Just as you wouldn't call using a calculator 'cheating' in maths, using AI for creative support isn't dishonest. It's about using available tools to create that spark... especially when time, energy or inspiration is limited.

- *Think of AI as a hyper-efficient brainstorming buddy.* AI can generate dozens of ideas in the time it takes to make a cup of coffee. It doesn't judge, hesitate or interrupt, which makes it perfect for rapid-fire idea generation, refining or reframing.

- *AI doesn't replace creativity... it enhances it.* You are still the storyteller. AI helps organise, expand or polish your thinking. But it doesn't replace your lived experience or emotional truth. It's the assistant, not the author.

- *Authenticity remains your responsibility.* AI can offer suggestions, but it's still prone to hallucinations and bias. So it's your job to filter, fact-check and decide what stays and what goes. You are always in the driver's seat.

- *Use AI like a creative partner.* Whether you're brainstorming holiday ideas or shaping a presentation, treat AI like a tool for your creative team. It is just one more voice at the table. Invite its input, but make the final calls yourself.

- *Let AI ride shotgun and never let it steer.* Inspired by Elizabeth Gilbert's *Big Magic*, I write a letter to AI: 'You're welcome on this road trip with Creativity and me, but you are absolutely forbidden to drive'.

PART II

Increasing your story intelligence

Now that you understand storytelling and why it's so effective, it's time to increase your story intelligence.

In this part, I will unpack a comprehensive storytelling framework, one I have been teaching for more than 20 years, so you can start crafting your own stories.

We'll begin by exploring the structure of stories at a high level...that is, using the basic framework of beginning, middle and end...and then go deeper into the elements that make stories effective.

Then we'll delve into the framework's key elements, which can either increase the effectiveness of your story or distract from it, and we'll look at the four types of stories you can share in various situations, before starting to find your own shareable stories. We're also going to put AI to work here as your creative partner, both to help you find more stories and to refine them without losing your authentic voice.

When people apply this framework to their storytelling it dramatically increases their story intelligence. This enables them to purposefully and skilfully use authentic storytelling to communicate with clarity and to connect, engage and inspire more effectively.

Ready?

The storytelling framework

5

Does your organisation refer to 'Our Story' when talking about its origins? Perhaps you have noticed that the 'About Us' section on its website has been replaced with the heading 'Our Story'?

When you read this apparent 'story', however, more often than not, it's only a timeline of events. They have called it a story even though it isn't one.

Or perhaps the 'story' is filled with jargon and vague company descriptions that sound impressive but say almost nothing concrete. For example, 'We leverage innovative, end-to-end solutions to deliver scalable, future-proof outcomes that optimise stakeholder engagement and drive strategic value to our clients'.

Calling something a story does not make it a story.

So what does make a story, a story?

The basics of a story

At a very basic level, a story needs to be about *someone* doing *something*. Something specific needs to have happened to someone because that results in us visualising the event, as well as making us feel an emotion. (Remember in chapter 1 we discussed that one of the reasons why stories are so powerful is because they tap into emotion and create a connection.)

I'm not suggesting a story needs to be about a hero's journey or have a Hollywood ending, but something needs to have *happened* ... to someone.

There needs to be some kind of specific event that helps people visualise and feel something that will create a connection and make the story memorable.

Some people make very generic statements and believe they are sharing stories. For example:

Growing up we moved countries a lot so I always felt like a bit of an outsider. But what this taught me was the importance of having the courage to always approach people to build connections because you never know where they will lead.

This is not a story, but it has the *potential* to be a story by adding a specific event that will help people visualise and feel something, such as:

Growing up, we moved countries a lot so I always felt like a bit of an outsider. I remember when I was about ten and started at a new school, I approached a few kids who were having lunch and asked if I could sit with them and they just looked at me and outright said, 'No'. So I just turned and walked away so they couldn't see the tears welling in my eyes.

I didn't let this experience stop me though. The next day I had lunch with a boy who ended up being a lifetime friend and was one of my groomsmen at my wedding last year. What these experiences taught me was the importance of having the courage to always approach people to build connections because you never know where they will lead.

Can you see that in the second example, with the specific event, you visualised something and you felt a connection, whereas the first example didn't do that for you. Or didn't do it as strongly.

You would have visualised something different from me, and that's natural. You can share a story with 10 people and they will all visualise something completely different. The key is to provide enough specific detail (but not too much detail) to allow people to visualise and connect with the story in their own way.

Once your story has a specific event, you can then structure this into a compelling story. Applying the proven storytelling framework described in the following sections will give you a greater chance of addressing each of the five criteria we discussed in chapter 3, which are:

1. *clarity:* the story is clear and logical

2. *engagement:* the story holds your attention the whole way through

3. *emotional impact:* there is a connection to the storyteller and their personal experience

4. *authenticity:* the story feels real and authentic

5. *memorability:* the message of the story is easy to remember.

Applying the storytelling framework

Remember Greek philosopher Aristotle and his model of persuasion of *logos* (logic), *ethos* (credibility) and *pathos* (connection) in chapter 1? Well, Aristotle has also been attributed to outlining the structure of a story. Around 350 BCE, he apparently said that for a story to be a story it needs a beginning, middle and end.

So let's start at the very beginning, because according to Julie Andrews in the *Sound of Music* 'it's a very good place to start'.

The beginning

The most efficient way to start your story is with one sentence that describes time and place. For example:

- *Growing up I was one of eight children.*

- *I started my career in the mid 80s as a trainee computer operator.*

- *Yesterday on a run I saw this woman do something very unusual.*

- *I met my husband Steve on a bike ride in my late 20s.*

What time and place signals to your audience is that you are about to tell them a story. And as human beings, we not only love telling stories, we love hearing them. We listen to stories differently, especially in business communications that could be a bit dry.

Imagine being in a meeting and your CEO is discussing the budget and then she says, 'This reminds me of when I was backpacking around Europe in my early 20s'. Your brain registers that you are about to hear a story. So you start to listen differently. This start to your story gets peoples' attention. It is often referred to as the 'hook' because it hooks people in.

Ironically, even though we love stories, you want to avoid starting your story with 'Let me tell you a story'. Can you feel the different physical reaction you have just reading this line? Perhaps you conjure up previous bad experiences of long-winded stories that don't go anywhere. You can think, and sometimes even say, 'Please don't; just tell me your point'.

If you have an inkling that your audience are 'get to the point' or 'just tell me the facts' type of people you *never* want to start a story with 'Let me tell you a story'. They will most likely shut you down before you have even started. I encourage you to still share stories, because if they are human, they will connect, but make sure you start with time and place and be super succinct (more on that shortly).

Notice that the beginnings I have suggested are not overly specific: for example, 'in the mid 80s' and 'in my late 20s'. Sometimes it may be appropriate to start your story with a very specific time frame and sometimes even a date … but it needs to be relevant.

For example, 'It was the 18th of March 2020 and I turned on the news to find out …' I can almost guarantee you that any story that starts with a date in March 2020 is going to be a COVID-19 lockdown type of story.

Sometimes being specific is important to the story; for example, 'On the day I turned 18 …' But if it is not important to your story, keep it general with phrases like 'growing up as a kid' or 'in my early 40s'.

In most instances, your beginning does not need to be any longer than one or two sentences.

The middle

While the beginning is typically short, the middle is much longer. As a bit of a rough guide, your middle should be about 70 per cent of your story, with the beginning 10 per cent and the end 20 per cent.

There are a few elements that take your storytelling to the next level. Let's explore them.

Name your characters

Sometimes your stories can be just about you, but usually they include other people.

When you introduce a key character you will be referring back to frequently, it is important to name them so the story is easier to follow.

For example, when I share a story about my husband or my daughters, I will name them: Steve, Alex and Jess. What I am not saying throughout my story is my husband, my eldest daughter, my youngest daughter, and so on.

If your story is about your favourite primary school teacher, name them. If it is about your first pet, name it. If it is about the first friend you had when you moved countries, name them.

The only exception to this rule is if your story is about your parents or your grandparents. Simply refer to them as you usually would: Mum, Dad, Nana, Grandpa, YiaYia, Nonna, and so on. I have shared many stories about my parents in this book and I only refer to them as 'Mum' or 'Dad'. If I referred to them as Margaret and Haydn it would seem unnatural as we usually don't address our parents by their first name.

If you don't refer back to the characters at all, then don't introduce them by name. One participant in a storytelling workshop started their story with 'Last year we went on a family driving holiday. I went with my wife, Jenny, and our three kids Ben, Maddi and Tim'. This sounds like a good start but he never spoke about them again because the main character was the mechanic, Harry. As he did not refer back to his family at all, a better start would have been 'Last year we went on a family driving holiday'. If it was important for the audience to get an idea of the age of the children, an alternative start could be 'Last year I went on a family driving holiday with my wife and our three young children'.

Keep your stories succinct

A common mistake I see people make when it comes to storytelling is that their stories go too long. If your story is going longer than two minutes, there's a real danger that your audience is starting to disengage. They will potentially start thinking 'get to the point'. The moment anyone starts thinking this, you are losing them. If anyone has ever said this to you, I guarantee you, they've been thinking it for a long time before they've said it.

Your stories will be more effective if you make them succinct ... 60 to 90 seconds when speaking.

I distinctly remember a general manager who was attending one of my storytelling workshops. His question was, 'When I share a story with my team, no-one tells me to get to the point. Yet, when I share the exact same story to the senior leadership team, people tell me to get to the point. I don't understand because it's the same story I'm telling.'

The imbalance of power in this situation means that the team that you manage are being very polite and not telling you to get to the point. When you are sharing it with people more senior than you, the power imbalance has shifted. This can be a real trap for senior managers. Always remember that you didn't get any funnier, you just got more senior.

Sometimes an effective way to share stories is to have several micro stories combined. For instance, you might be talking about exceptional customer service. You could share one longer story about what an employee did or you could share two or three micro stories to deliver the same message.

Express yourself

One way to make your story more engaging is to express how you felt. How did you feel at the time? Were you proud, disappointed or scared? And don't be afraid to share how you *really* felt... and I mean *really, really* felt.

I often have people in my workshops share a story and they may have said during the story that they felt anxious or a bit nervous. When I ask them how they really felt, they say something closer to the truth, such as 'I was so scared' or 'I have never been so bloody nervous in my life. I thought I was going to vomit'.

I am not saying to exaggerate, but if the truth is you were so scared you thought you were going to vomit, then say that as opposed to just nervous!

The ending

The ending of the story is the most critical part. It's a bit like landing the plane. It doesn't matter how smooth that flight was, the landing will make or break the flight. Similarly, your ending will make or break your story. It's the punchline to the joke. It's the 'so what'. It's the call to action.

The ending has three parts:

- the bridge

- the link

- the pause.

The bridge

The bridge is one sentence and can take many forms, but here are a few that work for me.

- 'I'm sharing this because it reminds me of...'

- 'The lesson I learned from that is the...'

- 'Reflecting on this reminds me of what we're trying to achieve with...'

The link

After the bridge, you move to the link. This is all about delivering your message without over-explaining it all. To prevent you from over-explaining try to make sure your link is no longer than two sentences.

Also, you don't want to end your story with 'The moral of the story is ... ', as that can come across as over-directive and, in some cases, condescending.

Try these links instead:

- 'Imagine what we could achieve if ... '
- 'Just think of what we could do if ... '
- 'I invite you to consider ... '

The pause

At the end of your story, pause for a moment and take a breath. It is only for a second or two but this is when your audience are connecting with the story. It is sometimes where all the magic can happen with stories.

Putting the framework into practice

Let's dissect the following story together, based on the framework.

(BEGINNING) *A few years ago, my daughter Alex introduced me to wine drops. I am not sure if you know about wine drops but they come in a tiny bottle and the idea is that you put five drops in your bottle of wine and it is meant to reduce the effect that the preservatives in the wine have on you.*

(MIDDLE) *So, last Friday, after a very busy week at work, I opened a bottle of red, added the wine drops, and poured Alex and myself a glass of Shiraz.*

When Alex went to the kitchen to refill our wine glasses, she picked up the drops next to the wine and asked, 'Mum, you didn't add this to the wine did you?'

I responded, a bit confused, with a yes.

Alex exclaimed, 'Mum, these are not wine drops. They are eye drops! You have poisoned us!'

Now, in my defence, the two bottles had a similar style, just different colours. But I made the assumption that they were wine drops because they were next to the wine. I made that assumption so strongly that I didn't even read the label. Mind you the eyedrops read 'Blink...Relief with every blink'. I think that even if I had read the label on a Friday night after a busy week, I could have easily thought it said 'Drink...Relief with every drink'.

(ENDING, BRIDGE) *I am sharing this with you because it highlights how easy it is to make assumptions.*

(ENDING, LINK) *While there was no harm done this time, it may always be worth stopping to check and read the fine print.*

(PAUSE)

Hold the mayo

The above is a great example of a story. But there is one special ingredient to a great story that you must always be aware of: being authentic.

We have already talked a lot about the general decline of trust in society and influx of fake news and AI-generated content.

We know it is getting harder to distinguish what is true and what is not. We know people deliberately tell false or exaggerated stories. (You probably know someone like that.)

You can't control what stories other people share but you can control the stories you share.

It's because of this I want to go a tad deeper on authenticity and the role of 'truth' in storytelling.

For you to be authentic in your storytelling, it comes down to two aspects. First, the story you're sharing needs to be congruent with your actions. This means you need to believe in the message of the story.

This is critical when you're sharing a story to communicate values. Whether you're talking about communicating values to your team, in a job interview or perhaps with your children, you need to actually believe in that. You don't want misalignment between the stories you share and what you do. If you're sharing a story about the importance of inclusion, then you want to be inclusive.

The second aspect of authentic storytelling is the story needs to be true. No making up stories; no exaggeration; no adding mayo (as we say colloquially).

'Don't let the truth get in the way of a good story' is a phrase often used humorously or ironically to highlight the tension regarding factual accuracy in storytelling. While it can have playful connotations, it also carries deeper implications about the nature of storytelling and the truth. And how embellishment, perspective or omission can shape a story's impact...and potentially the credibility of the story and storyteller.

Sometimes we are tempted to exaggerate details, dramatise events or add a bit of mayo. We think it will make our story more compelling. Some think that their original version of the story is not grand enough or engaging enough and that no-one would be interested in such a mundane, ordinary story.

There is real danger in embellishing stories. When you retell a story, you do not simply retell it; you relive it. By reliving the story, people can see your emotions. They might see pride, your eyes light up or your voice catch. When this happens, there is a greater connection between the storyteller and the audience.

The further you deliberately move away from the truth, the less that reliving will happen. You, therefore, run the very real risk of potentially losing your credibility because your audience senses it is not truthful. It might even sound too good to be true.

Remember, we are in a crisis of trust in the world right now. People are very sceptical, and the BS detectors are on high alert. When it comes to storytelling, you don't want to give people any reason to think your story is not true. Exaggerating even one detail could cast suspicion over your entire story and by default over you...because if you are lying about that, what else are you lying about?

However, there is a big difference between deliberately embellishing the truth and inadvertently getting a detail wrong.

For example, have you ever retold a story from your youth with your siblings, only for your parents to say, 'That didn't happen like that'? But your entire life, you've held a different version of events. That is your truth. Are you wrong and your parents right? Maybe. But the more likely scenario is that you each have a different recollection and therefore a different version of the truth.

While you should aim for accuracy in your storytelling, sometimes minor, inadvertent inaccuracies do not detract from the authenticity of the story.

Imagine you shared a story about the impact your basketball coach had on you. You talk about how he supported you and inspired the team. You recount a particular game when you were 26 points down at halftime, but with your coach supporting you and believing in the team, you went on to win the game by one point. That game had such an impact on you that you kept a copy of the scorecard to remind you of the important role your coach had on you.

What then if, two years later, you were moving house and you came across that scorecard and noticed that it wasn't 26 points down at halftime, it was only 22 points.

Factually, that story is now incorrect but the intent is authentic and that minor inadvertent factual error does not detract from the story. In addition, the reality is no-one except you would know about it.

So let me make this clear. I am not suggesting you should lie about the facts or deliberately exaggerate to make the story sound better, but if it's a genuine inaccuracy, it usually does not detract from the authenticity.

However, when it comes to inadvertent inaccuracies, you do need to be careful of them involving an event your audience will have knowledge about. You may be talking about a well-known event and if you get some information wrong (even something like the year it occurred) it can detract from your story.

Some people may not register the inaccuracy and some people may notice it but not care. But there will be some who notice the inaccuracy and it distracts them … and in my experience, they will come and tell you. Others may see this inaccuracy as a reason to doubt your credibility.

In any case, making up stories is a big mistake and can potentially damage your credibility and brand.

Let's look at some other common mistakes to avoid.

Common storytelling mistakes

These are three of the most common, yet avoidable, mistakes I see when people share stories.

Too many numbers

An aspect of your story that can negatively impact its effectiveness is including too many numbers. This can weaken the emotional connection.

For example, consider this start to a story.

In 1996, I turned 18. I did what any eager 18-year-old would do and got my licence that day. I was very eager to impress my new girlfriend. We had only been going out for three months. She was also 18 and had got her licence six weeks prior. So I drove to her house to surprise her. Her house was about 30 kilometres away. It felt so good because normally I needed to take public transport, which involved riding two buses, followed by a 15-minute walk...

Can you feel that this overload of numbers makes it hard to follow. Your brain has ticked over to logically following the story instead of just going with the flow.

A better version would be:

On the day I turned 18, I did what any eager 18-year-old would do and I got my licence that day. I was very eager to impress my new girlfriend, who had recently got her licence as well. So I drove to her house to surprise her. It felt so good to drive there as opposed to taking public transport like I had to do previously.

The second version is more concise and engaging while not being distracted by the numbers. I should say that if the information about the two buses and the 15-minute walk was critical to the story, then you would leave those details in.

Unnecessary detail

Besides too many numbers, another common mistake is too much unnecessary detail. For example, let's take the earlier example of not fitting in when growing up. Here is a version with too much unnecessary detail.

Growing up, we moved countries a lot so I always felt like a bit of an outsider. We lived in Australia, Singapore, the United States, a stint in Germany and then London. But I remember when I was about ten and started at a new school called St Columbus. They had purple uniforms, which I really didn't like...

All that content is not relevant to the story and it is also making it hard to follow. As the audience, I might be thinking that these details are important because they are included, but they are not. Of course, if it is relevant to the story that all those countries are named, by all means leave those details in ... but if not, omit them.

Every detail in the story should serve the story's purpose. When it comes to story intelligence, this discipline is really important. When crafting a story, you constantly need to ask yourself, 'Is this bit of information relevant or not?' If it is relevant, it stays in the story but if it's not, you have to have the discipline to omit it.

The way you decide on the detail to include or omit is by focusing on the message. What is the one single point you were trying to make with the story? If it is relevant to that message, include it.

If it is not, then leave it out. Including details that are not relevant will make your story go longer than necessary. They could also cause a distraction.

Real-time editing

What can also negatively impact a story's clarity is constantly editing your story. We all know people who do this. Please don't be that person. It sounds something like this:

Ten years ago, we went on a holiday to Vietnam ... actually, I think it was 11 years ago. No, wait, maybe it was longer than that ...

No-one cares!

Pick a time and place, and move on. Editing in real time is unnecessary and has resulted in your audience most likely switching off before you even get into your story.

If you have a beginning that starts with 'A few years ago' or 'In my early 20s, it will reduce the urge you feel to self-correct.

Follow the storytelling framework to avoid making common mistakes, and instead, increase your story intelligence.

If you share your story and you feel it doesn't work (and sometimes it won't), come back to this framework. Maybe your story was too long, or you left out some important details or you didn't quite land the bridge and link ... or maybe it was the wrong story for the message or audience. Simply rework your story or think of another one and give it another go.

People with high story intelligence consider a variety of stories depending on the reason to share the story and the outcome they want to achieve. So in the next chapter, we are going to look at the four different types of stories you should consider sharing.

That's a wrap

- *A real story is not a timeline.* Too often, businesses label something a 'story' when it's just a list of dates or corporate jargon. A true story involves something specific happening to someone and it makes people feel something.

- *Specificity creates connection.* Adding a clear moment, character or visual detail helps people see the story and feel its emotional impact. That's what makes it stick.

- *Use the simple yet powerful story structure.* Every compelling story needs a clear beginning (time and place), a middle (what happened, to whom, with emotional expression) and an end (bridge + link + pause).

- *Authenticity is non-negotiable.* Always believe in the story's message and keep it true. Even small exaggerations (or too much 'mayo') can erode trust... especially in today's sceptical world.

- *Avoid common storytelling traps.* Too many numbers, unnecessary details or real-time editing (like second-guessing dates) break flow and confuse listeners. Keep it short, sharp and relevant to your message.

- *Clarity, connection and credibility win.* Use the five criteria from chapter 3 (Clarity, Engagement, Emotional impact, Authenticity and Memorability) as your guide. Rework stories that miss the mark.

The four types of stories

6

Over the past 20 years, I have told and listened to many stories. I've come to realise and see that people with high story intelligence tell a variety of stories.

Some stories are lateral, which means they act as a metaphor or analogy of a similar situation. Other stories are literal, which means you have been in exactly the same situation.

In addition, stories can either be about firsthand experience, because you were there and something happened to you, or they can be based on secondhand experience, meaning it's something you have heard about or read about.

These stories can be classified into four key types (as shown in figure 6.1, overleaf):

1. *Personal stories*: stories of firsthand experience that are lateral

2. *Professional stories*: stories of firsthand experience that are literal

3. *Public stories*: stories of secondhand experience that are literal

4. *Parables*: are stories of secondhand experience that are lateral.

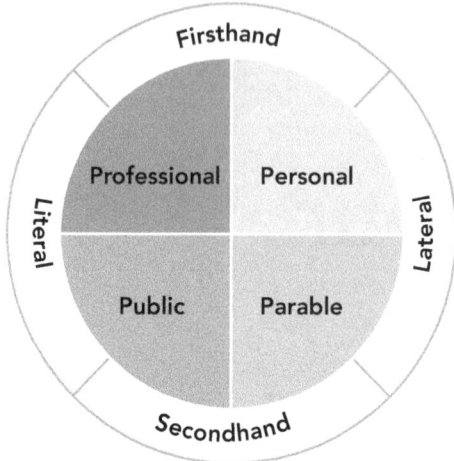

Figure 6.1   four types of stories

Each story type serves a distinct purpose, and when used effectively, they can create lasting impact. Let's explore them.

Personal stories

Personal stories share lateral, firsthand experiences.

What they are

Personal stories are drawn from your own life experiences. They could be the moments that shaped you, the challenges you have overcome or the triumphs you have experienced. Or they could be simple day-to-day stories of lessons you learned in a moment of time. Perhaps a bit of advice you received or a moment of regret. Even stories that seem unremarkable but show a snippet of your life and your values are personal.

Why they matter

Personal stories build authenticity and trust. They have the ability to fast track a relationship or strengthen an already existing relationship. When you share something about yourself, you invite others to connect with you on a human level. They can show your vulnerability and make you relatable.

Example

When I was 17, I was applying for full-time jobs. I went for an interview and felt it went okay.

However, on the weekend, I noticed the job was advertised again. I am showing my age here but this was when jobs were only advertised in the Saturday newspaper (I know, ancient I am).

I said to my mum, 'Obviously, I didn't get the job'.

She replied with, 'Obviously, no-one else got the job either', and she then suggested I apply again. It was a chance to write a stronger letter with everything that I had learned during the interview.

I was initially reluctant, thinking that would be really embarrassing but Mum convinced me to do it.

So I did. And I got a second interview where they asked me why I applied again.

I told them that I really wanted this job and I knew I would be good at it.

They offered me the job on the spot.

Thanks, Mum, for always encouraging me to give things a go … and if they didn't work out to then try something different.

Considerations

Personal stories are your most powerful stories, yet they are the most underutilised, especially in business. Some professionals think that sharing personal stories is not professional. Part of me suspects they are not prepared to share anything about themselves, or to show any emotion or still believe vulnerability is a sign of weakness.

This is flawed thinking.

While personal stories create an emotional connection, they are not about *being* emotional.

They are also not about you crying or getting other people to cry.

I came across an article where the author talked about the types of stories leaders need in business. One of the stories he suggested was 'The tear jerker' (seriously?).

If your starting point with stories is to make people cry, you are playing the game of emotional manipulation. This is wrong and it can very easily backfire as people can see right through it. Please don't do that.

Personal stories are also not about oversharing private details. You don't want to share a story and have people respond with, 'I can't unsee that'.

Not all personal stories need to show vulnerability (although the fact that you are even sharing a personal story in business can show a bit of vulnerability). If you are not familiar with the work of Brené Brown, then I highly recommend watching her TEDx Talk 'The Power of Vulnerability', where she states that showing vulnerability is a sign of strength, not weakness.

You can also use AI to develop prompts that help you find personal stories (more on that in chapter 8).

Professional stories

Professional stories share literal, firsthand experiences.

What they are

Professional stories are drawn from your work life. These stories showcase your expertise, values and perhaps leadership in action by highlighting lessons learned, successes, failures or pivotal moments in your career.

Why they matter

Professional stories build credibility. They demonstrate your experience and expertise. These stories should go beyond sharing facts and figures. They need to include emotions, lessons learned and the human side of work experiences, such as how you felt at the time (like pride or disappointment). They may also include quotes from other people like advice your manager gave you or feedback you received from a client.

Example

This is a story I often share when I am asked to be a guest on a podcast or panel and I share moments of my career, when things didn't go to plan.

> When I was about 35 I was doing some career planning and put in place a 5-year goal to be Head of Learning and Development at National Australia Bank. I completed an MBA part-time, put my hand up for any development opportunities and 5 years later found myself applying for the position.
>
> I had so many people tell me I was a shoo-in and I was quietly very confident.
>
> I didn't get the job!.
>
> I was really disappointed at the time but with a generous redundancy package on offer I thought I would have a go at teaching people storytelling. I had no idea if this would be a viable business option. I had never run my own business before

and I had never taught anyone how to tell stories either ... but I thought I would give it a go.

I felt like I had three things going for me.

Firstly, during my career I had designed and delivered a fair amount of leadership programs, so I knew I could design and deliver workshops.

Secondly, in my most recent roles as a senior leader and change manager I was realising the power of storytelling and believed it was a skill that could be taught and learnt.

Thirdly, Steve was earning good enough money to support us and that with the redundancy package gave us some financial freedom.

I also had the mindset that if the whole storytelling thing didn't work out, I would get another job. At least I would have had a couple of years at home with Alex and Jess.

It took almost a year to get the first client and the first few years were tough. But twenty years on it would be fair to say that it has worked out. My success has given myself and my family a life we could never have dreamed of. Plus, I have had the opportunity to work with some amazing people all around the world.

I am sharing this with you because sometimes the most pivotal moments in your career can be when things don't go as planned. And it's not what happens to you that counts ... but how you respond.

Considerations

When sharing these stories, avoid boasting and instead focus on lessons learned or moments of growth.

Also, avoid criticising previous employers or colleagues as this is never a good look.

Try not to make these professional stories feel like a case study, where you are just stating what happened. Talk about how you felt as well. For example:

- 'I felt extremely proud we were able to achieve what we did.'

- 'I felt really disappointed we were not able to deliver on what we had promised.'

- 'To this day it was one of the most exciting things that had happened.'

- 'I still reflect on that as it provided a very humbling learning experience for me.'

Notice how the words proud, disappointed, exciting and humbling create a connection over just stating factual information. Like personal stories, you can also use AI as a prompt to help find these types of stories. More on this in chapter 8.

Public stories

Public stories share literal, secondhand experiences.

What they are

Public stories are stories in the public domain. They are typically well-known stories or events from history, culture or current events. These include anecdotes about famous figures, historical moments, news stories, case studies or widely recognised phenomena.

Why they matter

Public stories provide a sense of familiarity and shared understanding. They're useful when you want to illustrate a concept or idea that resonates broadly. However, they lack the personal connection that comes with personal or professional stories, so they should be used sparingly and strategically.

Examples

Here I share one public story about the New Zealand All Blacks rugby team and one of my own.

Example 1

In James Kerr's book *Legacy*, he shares the lessons of leadership from the New Zealand All Blacks rugby team. One such lesson is the ritual of 'sweeping the sheds' after a game.

A couple of the most senior players grab a broom each and start sweeping out the change rooms or training ground, leaving them the way they found them…and sometimes in a better state.

This is an example of personal discipline and…not expecting somebody else to do your job for you.

They have a motto that no-one looks after the All Blacks. The All Blacks look after themselves. This teaches the players not to expect things to be handed to them. They believe that if you have personal discipline in your life, then you are going to be more disciplined on the field.

I think this is such a great example of respect and role modelling.

Example 2

This is a personal story of a holiday in Budapest that I often use at the start of my Powerful Presentation workshops. It's a good example of how you can take a public story and make it a personal story if you have a connection. The reason I'm sharing it here is because it is a public story. However, I have included my firsthand experience, which makes it a personal story and shows how your stories can be tweaked to suit different situations and needs.

On a family holiday to Europe a few years ago, we visited Budapest. The old Parliament building is one of the most amazing buildings I have ever seen. So we decided to go on an organised tour.

During the tour, we heard some pretty cool facts and some even better stories.

One such story was about the numbered brass cigar holders that sit outside the main chamber. During the era when smoking was allowed inside the building, but not in the chamber, politicians would often walk out of boring speeches and smoke their cigars while mingling and chatting.

Havanas were the popular cigar of choice. The holders were numbered so the politicians could safely leave their cigar in their allocated numbered slot and pop back into the chamber to see the start of the next speech. If the presentation was boring, they could easily return and identify their smouldering Havana.

In some instances, a speech would be so engaging that they would stay and listen to the whole speech and return to find their cigar slightly shorter. This resulted in the saying, 'It was worth a Havana', which was used to judge the quality of a speech.

What I hope for us to achieve in this workshop is to give you some insights, tips and frameworks to make sure that whenever you present, regardless of whether it is in person or virtually, to a few people or a few hundred people, that people walk away feeling that it was worth a Havana.

Considerations

While public stories can be engaging and familiar, they often lack the personal connection required to build authenticity and trust. We tend to default to public stories because they feel safe and neutral, but these stories often fail to leave a lasting impact because they don't reveal anything about the storyteller.

So it is best to use public stories sparingly and ensure they are clearly tied to the message or lesson you want to convey. Definitely avoid overused public stories and stories that have passed their use by date. As they are well known, and as we discussed previously, ensure what you are sharing is accurate.

AI can be really useful in suggesting a variety of public stories you can share for a specific message. You do need to check for accuracy and relevance, however, and we will explore that further in chapter 8.

Parables

Parables share lateral, secondhand experiences.

What they are

Parables, or fables, are short, fictional or metaphorical stories that convey a moral or lesson. They're timeless and often simple, making them easy to remember so are often used to make complex ideas more digestible. There are classic parables such as the story *The Tortoise and the Hare* and the parable of 'the boy who cried wolf' but be mindful that these can start to feel like analogies and clichés because they are so well known.

Why they matter

Parables simplify complex ideas and teach important lessons in a way that's accessible and relatable. While they don't reveal anything personal about the storyteller, they're powerful tools for teaching and illustrating key points.

Example

In the year 2000, I undertook an MBA in Management and Leadership. One of the subjects was 'Competitive advantage'. It was a relatively new term back then and the class were struggling to understand what it meant at a high level. The lecturer shared the following short parable.

> Competitive advantage is like two CEOs going for a walk in the woods when all of a sudden they see an attacking grizzly bear in the distance. The first CEO grabs a pair of runners out of their backpack and starts to put them on. The second CEO says, 'Are you mad? We can never outrun an attacking grizzly bear'. The first CEO replies with, 'I know, but I can sure as hell outrun you'.

Now, ignoring the ridiculousness that if a grizzly bear was running towards you that you would stop to put on runners, the message got through.

I would say that out of my entire MBA it is one of the few things I remember besides a SWOT analysis and Porter's 5 forces model.

Considerations

As with public stories, don't rely too heavily on parables. Because while they are memorable, they don't reveal anything about you personally or your experiences, which can weaken their impact when trying to build trust and credibility. And, like analogies, they can become cliché if overdone.

Parables can enhance a message, but they should not replace personal or professional stories. They work best as a complementary story.

As for public stories, AI will be extremely helpful in suggesting a variety of parables you could use.

So which type of story should you use?

Whether you're drawing on your personal experiences, professional challenges, widely known events or timeless parables, each type of story has its own unique power and serves a unique purpose:

- Personal stories build trust and emotional connection.

- Professional stories showcase skills and experience that can build professional credibility.

- Public stories inspire by drawing on universally known events.

- Parables teach life lessons in simple, digestible ways.

While public stories and parables have their place, they shouldn't overshadow personal and professional stories, which are more effective at fostering trust and connection.

When you share authentic firsthand personal and professional stories, people get to know you a bit better and this provides a significant added benefit because it can increase trust. These firsthand, authentic stories can strengthen an existing relationship or fast track trust in a new relationship.

Remember the research from neuro-economist Paul Zak that storytelling can trigger the release of the oxytocin 'trust hormone', resulting in a bond between the audience and the storyteller.

And, as we have discussed, in a world of distrust, any technique you can use to fast track or strengthen trust provides you with a great advantage. Imagine the power of fast tracking trust when pitching to a new client, in a job interview or speaking at an event. Or the benefits in strengthening relationships with your team, your ongoing customers or other key stakeholders. Your firsthand, authentic personal and professional stories have the power to do this, where secondhand public stories and parables do not.

All these types of stories are effective, but depending on your purpose for sharing the story, some will be more impactful than others. Regardless of the type of story, always tie it to your message or purpose. Make sure it resonates with your audience.

By weaving these types of stories into communication, you can engage, educate and inspire your audience effectively.

Understanding the four types of stories you could share is important.

We'll now begin to look at how to find stories. From my experience, people seem to struggle with finding their own personal stories. So, in the next chapter, I will reveal some different techniques you can use to help you find your own personal stories.

That's a wrap

- *Not all stories are created equal.* High story intelligence means understanding and using four distinct types of stories: personal, professional, public and parables... each with a unique purpose and emotional impact.

- *Personal stories are firsthand and lateral.* They are relatable, real-life moments that humanise you and build emotional connection. They're powerful but underused, especially in business, due to misplaced fears around vulnerability.

- *Professional stories are firsthand and literal.* They are grounded in your work experiences and lessons. They establish credibility and demonstrate skills and experience, but must go beyond facts to include emotional nuance and reflection.

- *Public stories are secondhand and literal.* They are widely known stories or events used to illustrate a point. They're accessible and familiar but lack personal connection, so they should be used sparingly and with a clear link to your message.

- *Parables are secondhand and lateral.* They are metaphorical, fictional or classic tales that simplify complex ideas. While they're memorable and easy to understand, they don't reveal anything about you, so they work best as supporting tools.

- *Mix, match and be mindful.* Use personal and professional stories to build trust and strengthen relationships. Use public stories and parables strategically to support a concept or message. Most importantly, always tie your story to your purpose and your audience.

How to find your own stories

7

Have you ever seen someone walking along a beach or a field with a metal detector on the hunt for something valuable? Looking for your own stories is similar. Your own stories are there, hidden just below the surface. And if you know where to look, you will detect some valuable stories to share.

At nearly every workshop I have conducted over the past 20 years (so that's a lot), I will inevitably have someone confide in me, 'I just can't think of any of my own stories'.

Over this time, I have uncovered some very effective ways to help people find their own stories without AI, and in this chapter, I will reveal them to make you a brilliant story detectorist.

This is your life

Imagine you were going to be featured on the TV program *This Is Your Life*, where the host takes you through all the significant events in your life. Let's do this process together.

I'd like you to think of one of your earliest memories and ask yourself, 'What was that about?'

My earliest memory was when I was about four. I recall being in the school yard. I can't remember if I had started school or was there with Mum to pick up my older brothers and sisters. But I can recall being with someone and she was swinging on a branch of a tree. So, I decided to join her. The branch wasn't very high above the ground (we were only four) but I remember swinging and I lost my grip and fell and cut my knee on a piece of glass on the ground. I still have the scar.

So what was that story about? Your initial reaction might be, 'Oh, it wasn't about anything', but let's challenge ourselves to think, what *could* it be about?

It could be a story about finding fun in the moment. Maybe it is about realising that everything you do in life carries some form of risk. Or it could just be a story about peer group pressure and following what someone else was doing.

In the end, you may decide that it truly was about nothing and it is not a story worth sharing.

But if you spend some time on this activity, what you are doing is starting to create a list of potential stories that you could use. The key word here is potential ... you will not use every story because not every story will have a reason to be shared.

When thinking through this activity, your natural tendency will be to automatically record the most significant events in your life. Examples may include moving countries, getting married, becoming a parent, changing jobs or breaking your arm.

When thinking of these events in your life, instead of thinking about these in general terms, try to be more specific. Some of my examples include:

- deciding to have children after going on a professional career development course (I know, weird)

- breaking my arm when I was 12 and not being taken to the doctor for two days

- getting married in a pub and wearing a black and gold wedding dress.

The more time you spend on this, the more potential stories you will uncover. Remember the metal detectorist. The stories are there. They are simply hidden below the surface. The best thing to do is grab a piece of paper and jot down any and all you can unearth.

During this process, you are likely to uncover stories that you have not thought of for years. You might have no idea of how you can use them but that's okay. There's a chance you won't ever use them, so all we are trying to do at this stage is capture them. Not all the metal you uncover will be precious, but you have to start searching to have a chance of finding anything.

For example, I have never shared the story of me falling from a tree and cutting my knee on glass because I just don't think it would deliver any message well enough. But, in an unforeseen plot twist, I ended up sharing the story in this chapter to highlight that not all stories are worth sharing!

If you spent only one hour doing this, I guarantee you will think of a handful of stories that you could share. The more time you spend on this, the more potential stories you will uncover. Or you could take this to the extreme, like one of my workshop participants did. Six months after the workshop, I randomly ran into her and she said, 'I am loving the "your life" activity you suggested we do. I am up to age 13'.

When you have exhausted this approach (and way before six months is up) you can start on the next step.

Flick through your camera roll

Next, grab your phone and swipe through your photos. You will be amazed at how some of those photos will spark a story behind the image. Your social media posts can also trigger similar memories.

I can recall working one on one with a CEO of a large health insurance company as he wanted to use personal stories to communicate his messages, but he was stuck on finding stories. My questions to prompt stories were falling flat so I suggested he pull out his phone and start flicking through his camera roll.

Within a minute he had scrolled past a photo of himself and his son camping and immediately thought of a story.

What does your camera roll tell you?

Check physical photo albums

When Jess turned 21 we did the standard photo wall. I did go through my phone and had a few photos printed but I also had photo albums for perhaps the first 10 years of her life. This was back in the day when the only way to see the photos you had taken on your camera was to get them printed (I know, I am ancient.)

Selecting photos brought back so many memories. I had no idea when or where some of the photos were taken, but many sparked stories. I ended up including one story in Jess's 21st speech because I think it perfectly highlighted one of her key values.

I encourage you to look through printed albums and journals for your own inspiration.

Ask people who know you well

I had one client who was enjoying finding his stories so much that he shared what he was doing with his wife. Consequently, his wife started to suggest all these other experiences he hadn't even considered. His list of potential stories grew exponentially!

Who else might you involve in your story-finding process? Maybe your parents, siblings, best friends or kids?

Consider specific questions

When we look for stories in our past, we usually skim across the surface and only see the most obvious memories, but there are often more stories to find. So once you have exhausted the options, work through the following questions to see if they trigger any more stories. Answer these questions from both a personal and professional perspective to potentially double the stories you will find.

- *Think about a time that made you feel proud.* What was it and why did it make you feel that way?

- *Think about a time that made you feel angry.* What was it and why did it make you feel that way?

- *What is something you are really embarrassed about and wish you had not done?* What was it and why did it embarrass you?

- *Is there a time in your life that you were given some advice and didn't take it?* Did it turn out for the best or do you wish you had taken it on board?

- *Think about a time you felt truly fulfilled.* What made you so content and happy? What were you doing? How did you feel? Why do you value this so much?

- *Do you have regrets in your life?* If so, what are they and why do you regret them? How has a regret changed the choices you've made? What would you do differently if given the chance?

- *Think about a time when you had conflicting values.* What did you do, and why?

- *Think about a time you were really apprehensive about doing something but you did it anyway.* What was it and why did you do it? How did you come to the decision to go ahead with it? What was the end result?

- *What values did your parents instil in you?* Provide a specific example of them teaching you a value.

- *Do you have a favourite teacher, coach or mentor?* What was the most significant lesson they taught you?

Collect stories while you travel

Once, while travelling in Europe, we stayed at a Citizen M hotel in Copenhagen. It was a funky boutique hotel that did things a bit differently. For example, the room key card was also a travel tag you could keep and use for your luggage. (Well, I assumed you could keep it, otherwise I'm guilty of having stolen it!)

The quote on the tag read, 'Always take home as many stories as you do photos'.

I believe travelling provides a good source of stories that you can use later in business because it provides new and different experiences. I know from my own experience that I always return from my travels with many new stories.

My advice for finding stories when travelling is as follows.

- When you come across something unusual, be curious and ask questions.

- Research the backstory when you get back to your hotel.

- Always reflect on how you could use that story as an analogy in business.

- Write down the story and take a photo so you remember it.

Once you are actively searching for stories, you will regularly think of more ideas to grow your personal story bank! Your best stories are inside you; you just need to start looking.

Now that we have explored how to find stories without AI, you're ready to look at expanding your story-finding abilities and using AI to help you. Let's really put AI to work!

That's a wrap

- *Build a personal story bank.* Use the 'This Is Your Life' exercise to revisit formative life events, both big and small. The goal is to gather a list of potential stories, knowing that not all will be usable but many will reveal hidden gems.

- *Use visual prompts.* Scroll through your camera roll or look through physical photo albums and journals. Images often spark vivid memories and stories that may have been long forgotten.

- *Ask those who know you best.* Sometimes the people closest to you, such as family, friends and colleagues, can remind you of stories you've forgotten or didn't recognise as meaningful.

- *Use thought-provoking prompts.* Answering reflective questions (e.g. moments of pride, regret or advice you ignored) can surface deeper, more emotionally resonant stories that connect with your values.

- *Always take home as many stories as you do photos.* Travelling offers rich, fresh experiences. When something piques your curiosity, investigate and reflect on how it might translate into a story you could use. Write it down or take a photo to jog your memory later.

Putting AI to work, smarter *and* harder

8

So how can you use AI as your creative partner, specifically for your stories? Let's use it to help you not only find your stories but refine them, too.

Remember the four types of stories described in figure 6.1? Let's look at how you can use AI to help write each type.

Putting AI to work on personal and professional stories

When I started writing this book in late 2024, my premise was that AI is super effective for helping you find public stories and parables. However, I believed its effectiveness was limited for finding personal and professional stories. This is because these are your own stories and not stories that are in the public domain. (Although I'm sure it will only be a matter of time before you can ask AI to mine your social media accounts and suggest a story.) Regardless, the very nature of these learning models is that they keep learning... and getting better.

Six months after starting to write this book, my premise had changed. As I have been experimenting with AI to help me find and refine stories, I have come to the conclusion, as you are about to experience, that AI can be very effective in helping you with your personal and professional stories, too.

The place to start is by asking AI to ask you questions.

Using AI as my creative partner, I entered the following prompt in ChatGPT:

Can you ask me some questions that will help me uncover my own stories?

I was pretty impressed by some of the questions that were generated, so I have included them here for your benefit. But I encourage you to do this yourself. The cool thing about Gen AI is that the different forms of Gen AI won't give you the same response, even if you type in the exact same prompt (it's not a Google search).

What is your happiest memory? Describe the event, who was involved, and what made it so special. How does it shape your current outlook on life?

Have you ever experienced a moment of failure? Reflect on a time when things didn't go as planned. What did you learn from that experience, and how did it change you?

What is a risk you took that paid off? Share a story about a time you stepped outside your comfort zone. What were you afraid of, and what was the outcome?

Who has had the most significant influence on your life? Think about a mentor, friend or family member. What lessons did they teach you, and how did they impact your path?

Have you ever made a promise that you couldn't keep? Describe the situation and the reasons behind it. How did it affect your relationships or your sense of self?

What is the craziest adventure you've ever been on? Think of a trip or an experience that was out of the ordinary. What challenges did you face, and what did you take away from it?

Have you ever travelled somewhere that changed your worldview? Describe the place, the culture and the experiences you had. How did this travel influence your thoughts or beliefs?

What was your first job, and what did you learn from it? Reflect on your early work experiences. How did this job shape your work ethic and career aspirations?

What is a cause or issue you feel passionate about? Describe your connection to this cause. Have you taken any actions related to it? Share an experience that highlights its importance to you.

What is something you've changed your mind about in the last few years? Consider a belief or opinion that has evolved. What prompted this change, and how does it affect your current thoughts or actions?

I'd encourage you to get specific with the prompts you use to see how AI generates questions for you to initially find stories and then refine your story.

AI in action

To showcase how this works, I used ChatGPT to help me write a story about embracing fear.

I started with an 'Ask me questions' style prompt:

Can you ask me some questions that will help me find personal stories about feeling fear and doing it anyway?

This gave me some fantastic, thought-provoking questions:

1. Can you remember a time when you said *yes* to a work opportunity (presentation, leadership role, big client pitch) even though you felt unprepared or terrified?

2. Have you had to make a personal decision (moving house, starting a family, sending kids off to something new) that scared you, but you knew you had to do it?

3. Was there a time when one of your children or family members showed courage that reminded you to face your own fears?

4. Think of a time when you tried something physically scary (paragliding, diving, climbing, even caravanning into the unknown!)—how did it feel before, during and after?

5. Have you ever travelled somewhere unfamiliar or outside your comfort zone, and fear almost stopped you from going?

6. Can you recall a time fear of failure or rejection almost paralysed you—but you acted anyway?

7. Was there a situation where you didn't have control over the outcome, but had to step forward despite fear?

8. Have you ever faced a health scare, financial risk, or personal loss that forced you to do things frightened but determined?

Would you like help turning any of your responses into a short story or keynote-style narrative?

I responded that I would like it to create a story about when I went tandem paragliding and asked what it needed from me.

ChatGPT came back with some specific questions for me to answer such as:

- Where were you when you did the paraglide?

- Why did you decide to do it?

- Was there a moment you almost backed out?

- What do you remember about the moment before you started running?

- What did it feel like in your body as you ran off the edge?

- What did your tandem instructor say or do that stuck with you?

- What was your first thought or feeling once you touched down safely?

In answer to those questions, I shared the following information with ChatGPT.

Steve and I were in Turkey with friends and one of our friends really wanted to do it so I said I would do it with him.

The ride up the mountain was treacherous and the driver seemed very distracted and there were many times I thought he was going to drive over the edge of the mountain.

Even though I was getting unbelievably nervous I knew I couldn't chicken out because the thought of driving down the mountain with this maniac driver was more terrifying.

We got to the top and with the wind picking up the instructor pointed to Russell and myself and said, 'You two are first let's go.'

It all happened really quickly but I still remember him saying, 'run and don't stop running until I say stop.'

I did and the next thing I knew I was running but there was no ground underneath me.

I remember the utter relief on Steve's face when I landed.

From this information, ChatGPT created the fleshed-out story below:

Steve and I were in Turkey with friends when one of them suggested we go tandem paragliding. Now, I hadn't exactly gone to Turkey with that in mind, but when our mate Russell said he was doing it, I found myself saying, 'Sure, I'll do it with you.'

The real fear, however, began on the way up. The ride to the top of the mountain was terrifying. The driver was swerving dangerously close to the edge while also seeming completely distracted. I spent most of the trip clutching the seat in front of me, convinced we were going to tumble off the side. The irony was, by the time we reached the top, the thought of driving back down with this maniac behind the wheel felt even scarier than jumping off the mountain.

When we got to the top, the wind had picked up, and before I had time to think about it, the instructor pointed straight at Russell and me. 'You two are first. Let's go.'

It all happened so fast. I remember the instructor shouting, 'Run! Don't stop running until I say so.' And I did. Only suddenly, there was no ground under my feet. One moment I was sprinting, the next I was suspended in the air, the earth dropping away below me.

The flight itself is a blur, but what I remember most is the look on Steve's face when I landed safely. It wasn't just relief—it was the kind of expression that said, 'Thank God you made it.'

That experience taught me something important: sometimes fear tricks us into thinking staying put is safer than leaping. But in my case, the scarier option was *not* jumping. I'd rather run off a mountain into the unknown than stay stuck in a dangerous situation. And in life, I've realised it's often the same—the risk of change is usually less terrifying than the cost of staying where you are.

It would be fair to say I was pleasantly surprised with ChatGPT's end result ... and surprisingly how accurate all the additions were. Of course, if the additions were not accurate, you would omit or change them to reflect what really happened.

I was also impressed with the bridge and link at the end of the message. And I totally agree with the sentiment that the risk of change is usually less terrifying than the cost of staying where you are.

Suggested prompts

Here are some suggested prompts to get you started if you haven't done this before.

I need to give a speech for my daughter's 21st and want to include some short stories. Can you ask me some questions to help me find these stories?

I want to write a card to my friend, whose father recently passed away and I want to include a story about him. Can you ask me some questions to help me find these stories?

I want to talk to my team about the importance of collaboration and want to share a story to get that message across. Can you ask me some questions to help me find these stories?

I have a big sales pitch to deliver and want to share both personal and work stories around the value of sustainability because that is very important to the client. Can you ask me some questions to help me find these stories?

A word on the quality of your prompts when using AI: they are important. The more specific and clear your prompt is, the more useful the response will be. It may take some time to learn what works best. If you're not happy with the response you receive from AI, just ask again with a more specific prompt.

Putting AI to work on parables and public stories

Let's explore how AI can be used to find parables.

Previously, I shared a parable around competitive advantage about two CEOs walking in the woods and coming across an attacking grizzly bear. Say, for example, you wanted to find a parable on this topic.

To demonstrate, I opened up ChatGPT and Claude and typed in the following prompt:

Can you tell me a parable about competitive advantage?

Claude's response was:

In a lush valley between two mountain ranges, there lived two merchants who sold water to travellers crossing the desert. Both merchants had established their wells near the same dusty trade route, but their approaches to business were dramatically different.

The first merchant, named Ravi, always sold water at the standard price. He kept his well simple, with a basic bucket and rope, and relied on the fact that travellers needed water to survive. 'Water is water,' he would say. 'People will buy it no matter what.'

The second merchant, named Zara, took a different approach. She saw the same water not just as a necessity, but as an opportunity to create value. She built a small rest area around her well, with shade from date palms, comfortable sitting stones and clean cups. She cooled her water with clay pots and added mint leaves, making each drink refreshing and memorable.

Travellers who reached Zara's well would pay twice the price Ravi charged, but they did so willingly. Her water wasn't just water—it was an experience. Weary travellers didn't just quench their thirst; they found momentary relief from the harsh desert, a brief respite that felt like an oasis.

As seasons passed, Ravi's customers became fewer. Travellers would go out of their way to reach Zara's well, even if it meant walking extra miles. They would tell stories about her remarkable way of serving water, spreading her reputation far and wide.

Ravi couldn't understand why his business was struggling. 'I'm selling the same water!' he would complain. But Zara understood something fundamental: in a world of commodities, true value comes from how you deliver, not just what you deliver.

The moral of the story is simple: competitive advantage isn't about having something others don't—it's about doing something others won't. It's about transforming the ordinary into the extraordinary and seeing potential where others see only the standard.

It's a good story, but I wanted to check for accuracy, so I asked Claude to tell me the origin of this parable and the response was:

I apologise, but I want to be transparent that this is an original parable I created specifically for our conversation. It wasn't drawn from an existing traditional story or folklore. Would you like me to suggest some legitimate parables?

I admired Claude for its honesty and responded, 'Yes, please' and then received a few examples of legitimate parables.

To contrast and compare, I then opened ChatGPT and entered the same prompt:

Can you tell me a parable about competitive advantage?

ChatGPT's response was:

Once upon a time, in a dense forest, there lived a fox and a hedgehog. The fox was clever and quick, known for her cunning strategies and ability to adapt to any situation. The hedgehog, on the other hand, was slow and steady, known for doing one thing exceptionally well: rolling into a tight, impenetrable ball when danger appeared.

One day, as the sun set over the forest, the fox spotted the hedgehog foraging for food. With a sly grin, the fox thought, 'This will be easy. That little creature doesn't stand a chance against me'.

She crept closer, silently planning her attack. With a sudden leap, the fox pounced, her sharp claws aimed at the hedgehog. But in the blink of an eye, the hedgehog curled into his defensive ball, his spines pointing outward like a fortress. The fox recoiled, frustrated and a little embarrassed.

Determined not to be outdone, the fox tried again. She circled the hedgehog, darted in and out, and even pretended to walk away before lunging unexpectedly. Yet, every time, the hedgehog used the same simple strategy: he curled into a ball and waited. No matter how clever the fox's approach, she couldn't penetrate the hedgehog's defence.

Exhausted and defeated, the fox finally slinked away. The hedgehog uncurled, shook off the dust, and calmly continued his search for food.

The animals in the forest watched this exchange and learned a valuable lesson: true strength doesn't always lie in doing many things; sometimes, it's about mastering one thing that sets you apart.

The hedgehog's competitive advantage wasn't speed, agility, or a clever trick—it was his ability to focus on what he did best and do it flawlessly. The fox, with all her brilliance, lacked that single, defining edge.

And so, the forest remembered the tale of the fox and the hedgehog: in a world of many options, a clear and focused strength can be your greatest advantage.

The moral: to gain a competitive advantage, identify what you do best — something others can't easily replicate — and commit to it with confidence and consistency.

I asked ChatGPT for the origin of the story and it advised me that it originated from an ancient Greek poet called Archilochus. ChatGPT also advised me that the parable has been used in more recent times, specifically by Jim Collins in his book *Good to Great* where he called it the Hedgehog Concept.

Not totally trusting AI, I then researched this parable to make sure it was true and accurate. It is important for you to check for accuracy, because if you tell that parable about the two merchants selling water to travellers and people ask you where it came from because they have not heard it before, what do you say?

If AI made it up and you are using it, that will reflect badly on you. Best-case scenario it comes across as lazy. Worst-case scenario, you lose credibility. That is story stupidity, not story intelligence.

Remember: Do not let AI take control of the steering wheel. When using generative AI to help with your stories, you always need to check for accuracy. *Always!*

Let's play the same game with public stories. I went back to ChatGPT and Claude again with the following prompt:

Can you provide some real-life examples in business of competitive advantage?

They both provided a similar list of examples, including Apple's products, Amazon's logistics, Netflix's content and Coco-Cola's brand and distribution.

Neither produced a story, but each gave me a starting point to explore further. And, in fairness, the quality of my prompt was not very specific. And as we know, the quality of the prompt is important.

If you are not happy with the responses you are getting from AI, either ask for more examples or change your prompt.

For example, I recall hearing a story about Steve Jobs dropping the original prototype of the iPod into a fish tank to show that there was room for improvement. So I asked ChatGPT about it, using the following prompt.

Can you relay the story about Steve Jobs dropping the original iPod in a fish tank to show there was room for improvement?

ChatGPT's response was:

The story of Steve Jobs and the fish tank test is one of the most famous examples of his relentless pursuit of perfection. It happened during the development of the original iPod in 2001, showcasing Jobs' extraordinary attention to detail and his knack for pushing teams beyond their perceived limits.

The story

Apple's engineers had been working tirelessly on the first iPod, a groundbreaking device that would forever change the music industry. When they finally presented the prototype to Steve Jobs, they expected him to be impressed. After all, it was an engineering marvel — compact, functional and elegant.

Jobs held the prototype in his hand, turning it over and examining it carefully. Instead of praising their work, he frowned. 'It's too big,' he said flatly.

The engineers, somewhat taken aback, pushed back. They explained that the device was already as small as it could possibly be, given the technology available at the time. Every millimetre of space had been used for the hard drive, battery and circuit boards. 'We've packed everything in,' they insisted. 'There's no way to make it smaller.'

Jobs wasn't convinced. In a moment of theatrical genius, he walked over to a fish tank in the room and dropped the iPod prototype into the water. As the device sank to the bottom, tiny air bubbles began to rise to the surface.

'There,' Jobs said, pointing at the bubbles. 'That means there's space in there. Make it smaller.'

The Lesson

Jobs' dramatic demonstration wasn't just about shrinking the iPod—it was about challenging assumptions. The bubbles symbolised the potential for improvement, a reminder that what seemed impossible often just needed a fresh perspective and more determination.

This moment became a hallmark of Jobs' leadership style. He was never afraid to push his team to go beyond their limits, even when they thought they'd reached the boundaries of what was possible. His insistence on making the iPod smaller wasn't about micromanagement—it was about delivering a product that felt impossibly sleek, something no other company could match at the time.

This example illustrates the need for carefully checking for accuracy. When I originally asked that question, I mistakenly referred to the iPad instead of the iPod. ChatGPT responded with the same story but used iPad instead of iPod. It was only on reflection that I remembered it was the iPod that was the product in this example. I checked other resources and found that it was in fact the iPod. Intrigued, I went back to ChatGPT and asked it for clarification on whether it was the iPod or iPad.

ChatGPT came back with full disclosure to say that it was the iPod and it had used iPad because that is what I asked for. Prompts are important! So, too, is fact-checking from a variety of sources! Remember the very eager librarian that will make up stuff, in its eagerness to please if it doesn't know the answer.

Putting AI to work to refine your story

As well as using AI to find your stories, you can put it to work to help you refine your stories.

You could use AI to improve all aspects of your story. Here are some suggested prompts to consider:

Edit this story for spelling and grammatical errors only.

Check for structure and clarity of message and suggest improvements.

Summarise this story down to 300 words.

Tailor this story for an audience of CEOs.

Tailor this story for an audience of graduate students.

Ask me questions about my story that help me uncover why I made that decision.

As I have mentioned, the landscape of AI is changing at a rapid rate, with new players entering the market constantly. I encourage you to experiment with different AI platforms as they have specific areas where they excel. For example, at the time of writing this book, I was predominantly using ChatGPT for idea generation and both ChatGPT and Claude to help me refine my stories.

Other platforms can turn text into images and videos, so you could even use AI to turn a story into a video.

Remember, when using AI to help refine your stories, ensure it doesn't:

- strip out too much specific detail

- insert unnecessary analogies

- remove information on how you felt

- bring in cliché statements

- overuse the em dash — what is it with AI and the em dash? See what I did there? Look at any AI-generated content and you will see more em dashes in a few paragraphs than you have probably used in your life (with the exception of all the professional writers and editors who have legitimately and accurately used em dashes their whole career and are saddened by how AI has tainted their em-dash friend).

Other things to consider when using AI

Besides all of the above and checking for accuracy there are other things you need to consider when using AI to help with your stories and to make sure you well and truly still have control of the wheel.

Maintain your voice

Have you noticed an influx of AI generated content on platforms such as LinkedIn? This includes posts and comments. Many are saying that it is decreasing the value of LinkedIn and many people are turning off because of that.

The reason is because it's starting to all sound the same. It's important to keep your unique voice and not contribute to the rise of beige, bland and boring.

When you use AI to help you generate content, it is important to review and rewrite as appropriate in your voice. As AI gets more sophisticated, it will learn how to 'speak' in your voice, but you should still review this.

A good technique to ensure your unique voice is maintained when using AI is to actually say the story out loud. As you do this, you will know whether it sounds like you or not. It could just be a word that you would never use ... so change it.

Personalise the story

Wherever possible, your stories will be more effective if you can personalise them. For example, you might find a great parable in a children's book that you could share, but you could personalise it by saying that it was a book you used to read to your children, or your parents used to read to you (if that's true, of course).

The competitive advantage story I share about two CEOs coming across an attacking grizzly bear is a parable that has been personalised because I explained how I heard the story from my university lecturer and the impact it had on me.

This chapter has shown how you can use AI to find stories and to also refine your stories. In part III, I'll showcase a variety of stories that people have shared, the results they achieved and why the stories worked.

That's a wrap

- *Use AI as a story-finding partner.* AI can help you uncover personal and professional stories by asking thoughtful, tailored questions. You can prompt it with general or specific themes to help uncover experiences worth turning into stories.

- *Refine, don't copy and paste.* While AI-generated drafts may be compelling, they often include inaccurate or embellished details. The key is to edit AI output by adding missing truth, deleting inauthentic moments and personalising it so the final version reflects reality.

- *Prompts shape results.* The specificity of your prompt directly influences AI's usefulness. Clearer prompts generate more focused and relevant results. If you're not satisfied, reword the prompt.

- *Fact-checking is essential.* AI excels at generating parables and suggesting public business stories, but fact-checking is essential. Misinformation or invented stories can damage your credibility if shared without verification.

- *Use AI to edit and refine your stories.* You can ask AI to polish grammar, condense word count, adapt tone for a specific audience or improve narrative flow.

- *Maintain your voice.* Always review AI-generated stories to ensure they sound like you. Avoid falling into the AI-blandness trap where content sounds generic. Speak your story aloud to see if it still feels personal and true…then revise accordingly.

PART III

Sharing your stories

I know from experience that providing examples of stories helps people understand what makes a good story and where they can share them.

So for this part of the book, I asked friends, colleagues and clients to submit personal and professional stories they have used, and also where they have used them. The vast majority said they shared them in more than one scenario. For example, in a presentation, but also in a newsletter.

I am a proponent of the concept of creating once and delivering often. I will often record a story on my phone and share the video on social media. If it's appropriate, I'll then write the story up and share it in my newsletter and in a LinkedIn post. Many times, those stories find their way into a podcast episode or a keynote or a workshop . . . or all three.

I have placed each story where I think it fits best, but the reality is they can all be shared in many different scenarios.

I deliberately chose a variety of stories. Some are quite humorous and others are quite sad. Some are about a relatively common everyday event and others are about traumatic, life-changing experiences.

In any case, I hope that part III of the book inspires you to share your stories in multiple ways. Enjoy!

Stories for presentations

9

'Mum, can you help me with my assignment?' is a question I didn't hear that often when Alex and Jess were at uni. Especially from Jess, who was doing Agricultural Science at Melbourne Uni...I can't say Ag Science is my strength.

So when she did finally ask me this question, it seriously came as a surprise.

Part of her assignment was to deliver a five-minute presentation, and the lecturer told the students to make sure the presentations were engaging and to tell a story. (Now, *that* I can do!)

Jess thought, 'I know someone who can help me with that'.

According to the brief, Jess had to present on the relationship between an animal and their handler, specifically the pros and cons for each. Jess chose the relationship between border force security and the border force dogs they use, the Labrador Retrievers.

She had five minutes, which I determined was two minutes to talk about the pros and two minutes to present the cons, which left us a minute to top and tail it.

I suggested she start with a personal story on why she chose that dog or maybe even a 'fun fact'. Jess told me she had found out that sniffer dogs were first used by police to try and find Jack the Ripper (*wow!*). But then she said, 'Mum, don't forget it's for uni so it has to be *serious*'.

And this is where so many presentations go wrong…

Just because it's 'uni'…or 'business'…or 'finance'…or 'technical'…or 'compliance'…or *'serious!'*…we think it can't be engaging or, dare I say, entertaining… *big mistake.*

No, you don't have to do a stand-up comedy routine, but your presentations need to be engaging. If they are not engaging, then you are not getting your audience's attention, which means your audience will not remember a thing you said.

When Jess gave me her presentation script to review I had a very proud 'Mum' moment.

> *Let me take you back to the year 1888. There is a serial killer on the loose who goes by the name 'Jack the Ripper', terrorising London citizens, and police are stumped. They have exhausted all their attempts in trying to find this violent, bloodthirsty criminal, yet have failed each and every time. And while the killer was never caught, police used a new technique of trying to track down the murderer: the sniffer dog. And that was the very first time sniffer dogs were ever used as a tool by police.*

Now, I don't know about you but I am paying attention for the next four and a half minutes. Jess also advised me that she scored quite highly for that assignment and had lots of comments on the effectiveness of her story.

So let's look at other examples of shared stories that make presentations engaging and impactful. Then you can craft your own!

The bucket has moved

Nicky Berger is a farmer from New Zealand who attended one of my storytelling workshops in 2016 and said it 'radically transformed the way I communicated across a number of roles'. Nicky had to present to a large group of corporate agriculture professionals, and her main message was about reassessing where valuable resources and energy are allocated. In addition, it was her first time presenting to a large audience. So, as you can imagine, she was very nervous.

The story

When our children were little, we kept a food scrap bucket in the corner of the kitchen floor to make it easy for them to put their mandarine peels, apple cores, etc. in for composting. This placement suited them, and they were very good at aiming their food scraps from a reasonable distance.

One day, when I thought the kids were old enough, I moved the bucket to its rightful place, inside a kitchen cupboard. It was amusing that in the following weeks our kids continued to throw their peels and cores onto the floor in the corner of the kitchen, rather than into the bucket in its new home. Even though the bucket had moved, they were still aiming at the same place they always had.

Sometimes, I can't help but feel our agri-industry has a similar outlook: we aim our resources, we focus our energies, where we've always focused them. Whether that is our wool industry, the food or fibre that we choose to produce on our land, or whatever we consider the biggest risk to our future prosperity. However, at some point it would be good to stop, pause and realise, that just maybe, the bucket has moved.

The result

Nicky said that the audience wasn't expecting a speech from a farmer to start this way, so they found it surprising and amusing. She found it was a great way to relax into the rest of her speech because it gave her confidence that she could offer something that they didn't already have.

Why it works

The start of the story captures you immediately and creates a strong visual. The simplicity and succinctness of this story make it effective. It shows that you can take a really simple story about kids throwing food scraps into a bucket and link it to something much more significant.

How much for your lollies?

The next story comes from Lynne Storey-Naphtali, whom I first met when I conducted storytelling workshops for Accenture. I related to her immediately (and not only because she has 'Storey' in her name).

Lynne shared that when she was a commercial director for a major banking client she was asked to present at their account-planning week. Lynne was assigned the graveyard shift … the last presentation on the final day. This is a hard gig as you are literally the only thing standing between your audience going for a drink or going home.

To make matters even more challenging for Lynne, she had to present on pricing. She knew this would be a hard sell to the accounts team, and she was concerned that everyone would have switched off by the time of her session.

She knew a story was her best chance of engaging her audience, so she decided to include a relevant personal story about pricing that would have an impact and be memorable.

She planned her story to be at the start of her presentation and included a relevant photo. All slides had to be submitted beforehand, so she knew there was no backing out.

As she rose from her seat to speak, a larger-than-life picture of her son Harry and his cousin Elijah, with huge smiles on their faces, was projected on the screen. At this point, silence descended upon the room. Lynne took a deep breath and began.

The story

My son, Harry, was in Hong Kong visiting his cousin Elijah for a surf camp.

Every day, they would take the ferry from the mainland and back again. In the morning, they could buy lollies on the ferry, which was a popular activity among the surfing crew. However, when they returned tired at the end of the first day, the shop was closed, making the ride home less fun.

On day two, Harry decided to mix things up. On the way out, he invested in quite a stash of lollies. Then, on the journey back to the mainland, when everyone was tired and undoubtedly in need of more sugar, he auctioned the lollies to the highest bidders. He was able to demand a higher price, since his goods were in demand.

He made a significant profit over the week, and the surf crew looked forward to the daily auctions.

This was only discovered by his Uncle David at the end of the week when a stash of cash was found in the boys' room.

I am sharing this with you because it relates to our pricing. Yes, we are selling more than just lollies, but the price we can demand for our services needs to relate to the demand and value of those services. Where we have a sought-after service, we can demand a higher price.

The result

As Lynne shared the story to the room full of executives, everyone was fully engaged. And as she moved on to the finer details of her presentation, there was a high amount of productive discussion in the room on how the team could adopt higher pricing for some of the services they delivered.

Lynne added, 'That day, I realised that putting myself out there with a story had paid off, and what could have been a forgettable session turned into something that was memorable for all'.

'Having a simple and memorable story to kick off my presentation demanded the interest and attention of the executive group and generated more discussion.'

Why it works

This is a great example of taking a simple story and linking it to something bigger. What Lynne has done well here…perhaps anticipating that her audience would be thinking, 'We are selling more important things than lollies'…is to call that out. If you anticipate this, then simply add a line such as 'I know what we are going through is far more significant than…'.

1 in 2.3 million

Karin Rex is the founder and owner of GeekyGirl in Florida in the United States and is often asked to speak at conferences about storytelling and data. One of her key messages is to emphasise that stories help people understand data better. She shared this story at a conference in Orlando, Florida.

The story

The odds of winning a 5-million-dollar prize in Florida's Gold Rush Limited scratch-off game are 1 in 2.3 million. Very few of us can picture these odds clearly. I know I can't.

For the human brain, numbers … whether very large or very small … are often challenging to envision.

When we share data like this, it's useful to help your audience envision that data using a relatable story.

How might we do that with this number?

Well, let's imagine you're at a fabulous conference here in Orlando (not hard to do, right?).

On the final night of the conference, you attend a networking event at Universal Studios. In Ollivanders Wand Shop you meet a potential client from Hamburg, Germany called Fritz.

You and Fritz bond over having kids with a similar taste in all things Potter and you each buy a wand. You end up hanging out together all evening with a few other colleagues. You enjoy some attractions, talk about business a bit and are excited about the possibility of working together. You even sit for a while and enjoy a meal. Afterwards, Fritz leaves to take a business call and you part ways. Unfortunately, neither of you had thought to swap contact details.

As you get up to leave the table, you notice that Fritz left his Ollivanders magic wand on the table. Those things are expensive! You decide to make it your mission to return it to him even though you only know his first name and the city where he lives.

So, instead of flying home to your own country, you fly from Orlando directly to Germany.

Once there, you rent a car and drive to Hamburg. You drive around the city for about 20 minutes and then decide to park on a random street. You walk down that random street for a few minutes and then stop at a random house and knock on the door.

Lo and behold, there's Fritz, so you give him his lost wand. Easy, right?

I'm guessing that most of you are thinking no way!

Me too. Let's explore why.

First of all, the population of Hamburg, Germany is 2.3 million!

Therefore, the odds of finding Fritz in the way I just described are 1 in 2.3 million!

So let me ask you a question: How many of you understand the odds of winning the lottery better now that you have heard this story?

The result

When Karin asks that question at the end, there is an overwhelming 'yes'. She then discusses why, and everyone agrees that the story gives the numbers meaning. The story allows Karin's audience to experience how a story gives meaning to numbers, which is more effective than simply telling them that stories give their numbers meaning.

Why it works

This story highlights how you can bring data to life with a story. It is through the story that the audience truly understands the 1 in 2.3 million chance. Karin uses the story and frames it so it's clear that it's not a true story by starting with the word 'imagine'.

And I love it because it is a great story about the power of storytelling.

My first car

Daniel worked for one of Australia's financial institutions as a people and culture business partner. He was invited to a town hall to talk to the bank's finance division about employee engagement and what it feels like to be engaged. The story he decided to share was this very succinct one about purchasing his first car.

The story

My first car I ever purchased was a 2002 Gold Kia Rio. The car was barely working: no working fuel gauge, hub caps zip tied to the wheels. You could even take the key out while still driving! It may have been far from perfect, but to me, this was perfection.

It gave me the freedom to be my best. I knew exactly what my car needed from me. I even packed jumper leads so I could help myself and other dumb 17-year-olds when their car battery died after playing music in a field at 3 am at a house party.

I was very clear on what I expected from this car and made sure I had the tools to get the most out of it.

I'm sharing this with you because it reminds me a bit of how we engage with our work. We are in a lot better condition than my old Gold Kia Rio. But we don't need to be perfect...we simply need to know our expectations, have the tools to do our job right and put in just as much as we get out.

The result

Daniel reported that he started to see people talk about engagement in their day-to-day language. He also added that for a while everyone in the finance division knew what everyone else's first car was. People would say, 'What's your first car story?' when talking about engagement.

Daniel said that the story helped take away the 'people and culture (HR) feel' that comes with engagement surveys, and made it real for people.

Daniel also said that 18 months after sharing the story they saw a significant uplift in engagement, and now are part of the Gallup Exceptional Workplace globally. He did admit that clearly those results were achieved by more than just the story, but he has no doubt the story 'made it real for people'.

Why it works

The pure simplicity and succinctness of this story adds to its effectiveness. The results of Daniel's story showed that people connected the message of employee engagement with their first car. And I have no doubt that the story did help with the significant uplift in engagement … granted I might be a bit biased.

That's a wrap

- *Stories make presentations engaging and memorable.* Even in serious settings like business, compliance or technical talks, without engagement, your audience won't retain your message.

- *Simple, personal stories can illustrate big ideas.* They can work whether it's a farmer's compost bucket showing misplaced priorities or a boy selling lollies to explain pricing strategy.

- *Stories help data and numbers come alive.* This is demonstrated in the relatable 'finding Fritz in Hamburg' scenario, which is used to explain 1-in-2.3-million lottery odds.

- *Well-placed stories build connection and spark discussion.* Opening your presentation with a strong story can relax you as a speaker and draw your audience in.

- *Even short, humble stories can inspire real change.* This can be seen in examples where stories influence workplace culture and audience perceptions long after the presentation has ended.

Stories for sales 10

People may believe they're making logical, fact-based choices, but beneath the surface, emotion is steering the wheel. This is especially true in sales. The best sales professionals understand this instinctively. They know that people buy based on emotion first and that logic follows later to justify that emotional decision (remember chapter 1?).

People will often talk about the importance of casual banter at the start of any sales meeting in an attempt to build rapport. And while this has merit, sharing stories is more powerful to build a connection than casual banter.

Victor Borge, who was a Danish and American actor, comedian and pianist, has been credited as saying that 'laughter is the shortest distance between two people'. But I think a good story can bring people together just as quickly. Stories are the quickest, most natural way to create an emotional connection and establish credibility. They allow people to see who you really are, what you believe in, and why they should trust you.

But there's an important caveat. Not every story is effective in a sales context. The stories you tell must be purposeful and authentic. Without intention, your stories may come off as irrelevant, or worse, unprofessional.

Regardless, whether you are selling yourself, a product or service, or attempting to get investment funding, stories can help in three specific ways:

1. *They can show how others have benefitted from your product or service.*

    This type of story is all about social proof. It's one thing to tell a potential client, 'Our product can help increase your efficiency'. It's another to say, 'One of our clients, in a very similar industry, reduced their processing time by 30 per cent within three months of using our system'.

    These kinds of stories help prospects visualise success and see themselves in the experience of others. They make the value of your offering tangible and real.

    Rather than simply listing features or benefits, bring those features to life through a story. Tap into existing case studies, customer feedback or workshop insights you've gathered. Add specifics, personality and detail. The more vivid and relatable the story, the more it resonates. For instance, when I sit down with new clients, they often ask about who I've worked with before. I'll deliberately choose examples that match their size, industry or challenges.

    Sometimes, I'll share a comment someone made during a workshop or talk about the transformation a team experienced after training. These real-world examples do more than inform … they reassure and inspire.

2. *They can demonstrate your values.*

    We often say we value things like integrity, customer service or trust. But in a world flooded with buzzwords and corporate jargon, these statements carry little weight on their own, especially in early meetings as you are most likely an unknown quantity to your client.

The fastest way to bridge that trust gap is to show them your values in action through a story.

Think about moments that reflect the heart of what you and/or your organisation stand for:

Why did you decide to join your organisation?

Can you recall a time when your team went above and beyond to fix a client issue?

What's something you're proud of in the way your company delivers its service?

Each of these moments is potentially a powerful story. For example, perhaps you joined your current company because you were inspired by how they handled a crisis with integrity. Or maybe you went above and beyond by driving across town with printed materials when a digital system failed just before a client presentation. These aren't just stories; these are your values in action and they're far more convincing than just stating your values.

3. *They can address potential concerns.*

This is mostly overlooked but arguably the most critical type of story in a sales conversation.

Most clients come into a discussion with silent doubts:

- Is this too expensive?

- Will it really work for us?

- We have tried this before and why is this different?

Rather than waiting for them to voice those concerns, or worse, ignore them altogether, you can proactively address them by telling a story.

This happens to me when I'm speaking with a potential global client who wants me to train their people on storytelling or presentation skills. They ideally want to conduct the training in person, but that's not ideal due to either budget constraints or the geographical diversity of the team. So they need to conduct the training virtually but have concerns about conducting a half-day workshop virtually.

The moment I sense this is a concern, I have several stories I can share to alleviate the concern. Here is the most common story I share.

It's certainly a valid concern as you have no doubt experienced some pretty ordinary virtual delivery... I know I have.

However, since COVID-19, when all training went virtual, I was determined to be the best virtual trainer in the business. I tested different techniques to ensure maximum engagement and it paid off. Since COVID-19, many of my clients still conduct their regular workshops with me virtually as the survey results show really high engagement.

I have even had one client say to me that my virtual workshop was the most engaging training they have ever done, and that includes in-person training as well.

Conducting the training virtually also allows me to role-model how to present more effectively in virtual situations. Because while it is harder... and it definitely is harder... that's not an excuse for it to be crap.

This kind of story does two things. First, it validates their concern and shows that I'm taking it seriously.

Second, it reframes the concern as something that has been successfully navigated before and is potentially a benefit to them.

Let's now look at how others have used stories in the selling process, either their products and services or themselves.

Minnesota Starvation Experiment

Alessandra Edwards is a performance and wellbeing expert who works with CEOs, senior executives and teams. Ironically, I first met Alessandra in the gym of a hotel we were staying at when attending the same course...hopefully that made a good first impression with a wellness coach.

Alessandra sends out a regular newsletter and it is one of the few newsletters I look forward to reading, predominantly because of her use of stories. While Alessandra sometimes shares personal stories, what she does well is share public stories to great effect. The following is an example of one of these public stories that she shared in her newsletter. And for reference, which will become apparent in the story, Alessandra is half Italian.

The story

In 1944, at the height of World War II, 36 young men in Minnesota volunteered for an experiment that would later become infamous in the world of nutrition science.

They weren't soldiers; they were conscientious objectors, and they agreed to be semi-starved under medical supervision in a nearly year-long study that became known as the Minnesota Starvation Experiment (not exactly the catchiest recruitment slogan. And let's be honest, there were definitely no Italians in that volunteer group. What can I say? We love to eat).

Their calories were slashed in half. They walked for miles each day. They were studied obsessively.

The result?

- *They didn't just get thinner. They got obsessed with food.*

- *They dreamed about meals.*

- *They hoarded recipes.*

- *Their mood tanked.*

- *Metabolisms slowed to a crawl. And when the study ended, most of them regained the weight, and then some, because their bodies were doing everything they could to survive.*

Why does this matter? Because nearly 80 years later, I see echoes of that exact pattern in my clients. No, they're not starving in Minnesota. They're not rationed or walking 20 miles a day.

But they are running businesses, raising families, navigating midlife bodies and trying to 'be good' about food (cutting calories, skipping meals, pushing through exhaustion) and then wondering why they feel flat, foggy, and obsessed with snacks at 9 pm.

Just like those men in the study, their bodies are doing exactly what they were designed to do: protect them.

Slow down metabolism.

Dial up hunger hormones.

Crank up cravings.

Because biologically, your body doesn't know you're 'trying to be healthy'. It thinks you're under threat.

And somewhere along the way, they wake up and find that their clothes feel tighter, their energy has dipped…and they're blaming themselves.

But here's the truth: you are not broken.

You're living in a world that makes it incredibly easy to gain weight and very, very difficult to maintain it.

Weight gain is multi-factorial: genes, sleep, stress, food environment, movement, hormones and more. But that doesn't mean you're powerless.

One of the most powerful things I teach my clients is how to work with these shifts instead of fighting them…through food timing, training styles and recovery.

Here's what I teach my clients:

- *Eat for glucose stability, not calorie restriction. Protein and fibre first, always. High fat and low carb works extremely well if metabolic disfunction is present.*

- *Prioritise muscle: it's your metabolic engine and your best long-term investment.*

- *Sleep isn't a luxury. It's a non-negotiable performance tool.*

- *Know your personal risk factors…genetic, family history or lifestyle…and work with them, not against them.*

- *And above all: drop the guilt. Replace it with curiosity.*

Your body isn't working against you. It's trying to protect you.

And when you give it what it needs…clarity, rhythm, nourishment, rest…it responds.

If your jeans feel tight, it might not be the dryer. But it's definitely not a failure.

It's information. And you can use it.

The result

Alessandra advised me that she has found weaving public stories into her content is one of the most effective ways to connect with her audience. She states, 'The feedback I receive often centres around humour and reliability, and this helps build trust and make the message stick. In a space that can feel clinical or prescriptive, stories create connection. They invite people to see themselves in the message, not just be told what to do'.

Why it works

Such public stories are informative and educate Alessandra's audience, which shows a level of care and effort towards her audience. They contribute to Alessandra's credibility as you can see that she researches what she is talking about.

Finally, this story works because it is always tied back to what Alessandra is offering without it feeling like a pushy 'sell'.

Treating the whole person

Suzanne Rath is the founder and CEO of a Cairns-based wellness practice called Wellness Embodied. Following is her purpose, or origin, story. It demonstrates why she is passionate about wellness and why she started her company.

Suzanne shares her story externally on her website, social media posts and industry publications as well as her various speaking engagements. She also shares this story internally with her team when discussing their vision and values.

The story

In 2013, I was working three physiotherapy jobs in Sydney and loving life. That all changed one sunny spring day when I was cycling home. I coasted downhill through a green light and out of the corner of my eye, I saw a car pulling across in front of me. Time slowed. I jammed on the brakes but then slammed face first into the side of the car.

As a physiotherapist of over a decade, I didn't think it was a big deal. My teeth felt loose, and I was mildly irritated by the amateur first-aider claiming I was in shock. I figured I'd be checked over in hospital and be on my way. The paramedics felt differently. They advised me that I had probably fractured my jaw, and there was blood coming from my ear, but not to panic.

I wasn't panicked.

In hospital, I ran nerve tests on myself as I impatiently waited to be seen. Seven hours later, I was discharged with a diagnosis of multiple jaw fractures and a surgery date for the following week with a surgeon called ... wait for it ... Dr Risk, who would be operating on me on ... would you believe it ... on Friday the 13th.

Surgery with Dr Risk on Friday the 13th ... seriously, you can't make this stuff up.

I figured it would be six weeks of healing, testing soup recipes and catching up on writing. I was blissfully unaware of what lay ahead.

Post-surgery, I woke in agony. Arch bars, which are tiny hooks embedded in the gums, held my mouth shut. I couldn't speak and relied on a whiteboard to communicate. My heart pounded, a throbbing headache set in and when the medical team came around, they spoke to my partner instead of me.

Still, I thought, once the fractures healed, I'd be fine. But at seven weeks, I was far from it.

Noise overwhelmed me, concentration was impossible and dinner with friends became an ordeal. I had to severely cut back on my work as my memory was terrible and I seemed to feel a constant sense of impending doom.

Doctors had no answers. An insurance-hired psychiatrist condescendingly diagnosed me with 'adjustment disorder', which is essentially struggling to accept my new reality. Now, I know this will sound ironic but I refused to accept that diagnosis. I felt I was not being heard and I wasn't being treated as a whole person.

So I built my own recovery team: an integrative doctor, a psychologist, physiotherapists, massage therapists and anti-gravity yoga eased my headaches for a short time.

I diagnosed myself with a post-concussion syndrome with ongoing effects from the mild traumatic brain injury. My GP agreed and, step by step, I made progress.

Two years later, I moved to Katherine and then later to Cairns, knowing no-one, but determined to build the clinic I wished had existed for me. A place where people feel heard and where we treat the whole person.

The result

Suzanne says the story demonstrates to potential clients that she has a lived experience of what they are going through. That the story helps them feel heard and understood. She has had many clients tell her that they attended the clinic because, via her story, they see that she has walked the walk. The story has also led to several paid speaking and workshopping engagements.

Why it works

Even though the story is about a traumatic incident, Suzanne uses humour to lighten the vibe. Enough time has passed for her to comfortably share the story. It doesn't come across as a hard sell but is more about her passion and why she started her own clinic.

Look who's crying now

I wanted to include a story in the sales chapter that was successfully used in a job interview because that's a situation where you are literally selling yourself.

Lauren Caffyn is my oldest niece and I have helped Lauren on occasion with some stories when applying for jobs. Several years ago, she not only wanted to change jobs but she also changed industries, moving from being a chef to becoming a prison guard. While she had no experience in this industry, she had experience in persistence and resilience, which was a key criteria for the prison guard role. This is the story she shared in that job interview.

The story

After I returned from New York, I took on a position as a chef at the Old England Hotel. Of 18 chefs, only two were female. It was an extremely challenging environment that tested my strength as a woman and as a capable chef.

I felt like the other woman and I were always getting a rough time from our colleagues. After a few months, I found out there was a bet going on among the males as to who could make one of the women cry first.

I was devastated, disappointed and angry when I found that out. It really did make me want to cry, but more than anything

I wanted to prove them wrong. So I worked harder than them, I stayed later to finish the clean-up and I came in earlier to do the prep for the day ahead.

While they were laughing and joking behind my back, I put my head down and showed them and my superiors what I was made of. I remember one night I cut my hand. It hurt so much it made me want to cry, but I just wrapped it up and waited until I was in my car on the way home to cry out the pain.

After three months of working hard with persistence and resilience I never thought I had, I was promoted above all of my colleagues to sous chef, which meant I was now their boss. Everyone was stunned. They didn't realise that while they had been busy joking, I had been busy working.

Although I could have paid them back for their antics, I didn't, because I knew that with persistence and resilience and the courage to keep going you can rise above trivial and inappropriate behaviour.

The result

Lauren got the prison guard job after sharing this story at her job interview and has continued to share that story to young females starting out in the prison system, which she says is equally as tough for women. Lauren reflects that, 'Women have to work harder to prove their capability at times and have to be mentally tough. So when they doubt themselves, I try to motivate them to push through and lose the impostor syndrome. Especially with women who are more than capable but still doubt themselves. I tell them they have worked hard to get a seat at the table, so take your seat … or build another table'. Wise words.

Why it works

The story is fast paced with only the necessary detail in that it engages the audience from the start and keeps them engaged. The simple mention of working in New York brings in credibility, which is critical in job interviews. In a testament to how powerful this story is, when I share this story in workshops, it often makes people start to tear up. And while this should not be the aim, it is an indication of its power.

Folding napkins and Swatch watches

Stéphanie Vilner-Sheppard runs her own consultancy called planetp, which is a global consultancy that adopts planet-centred design thinking to help companies innovate. Stéphanie often uses stories during the sales process. Here is one of them.

The story

When I was nine, I worked in my mum's family's business on farms and in restaurants in Switzerland. One of my jobs was to iron napkins and I used a steam press to iron and fold linen napkins. The whole time, all I really wanted to do was play with their German Shepherd dog in the garden.

So I invented a faster way to do my job by overlapping seven napkins and pressing them all at once. They came out perfectly, which was important because that Swiss family was really pedantic about the napkins.

One day, I was asked to go into the restaurant to say hello to a customer, and the next day, he returned and gifted me a Swatch watch. Too big for my wrist, he cut the strap down to size and said, 'I saw you yesterday with the napkins and I want to encourage you to always make time for inventing'.

It was one of the very first Swatch watches and I found out later the man was the founder of Swatch. This was over 40 years ago, and I've been innovating ever since.

The result

During a sales pitch, the client who heard her tell this story commented that Stéphanie must have a strong work ethic, having been 'put to work' at nine. Stéphanie then had an opportunity to talk about it being a question of purpose, and most kids are bored and have no purpose. She had an abundance of purpose, saying that it made her feel really useful. Plus she was getting paid by her mum's family, and of course she got to play with the German Shepherd.

Stéphanie got that client's consulting gig and worked with them for several years, and they constantly told her that they never forgot her Swatch story.

Why it works

This is a great example of how a succinct story can deliver a powerful message of innovation. Stéphanie wants her clients to know she brings an innovative approach and through the story she demonstrates that she has always been looking for better ways to do things.

That's a wrap

- *Emotion drives buying decisions.* People justify purchases with logic, but decide with emotion. Stories build authentic connection and trust faster than facts or banter.

- *Purposeful, authentic stories enhance sales conversations.*
  Stories must be relevant and intentional, otherwise they
  risk sounding unprofessional or distracting.

- *Stories help in the sales process in powerful ways.* They
  show how others have benefitted (social proof,
  relatable examples); demonstrate your values in action
  (credibility and integrity through real moments);
  and address unspoken concerns (validating and
  reframing doubts).

- *Public, personal and client stories all have impact.* From
  a newsletter story about the Minnesota Starvation
  Experiment to a CEO's personal recovery journey,
  stories humanise your message and differentiate you.

- *Short, memorable stories can create long-term impressions.*
  Regardless of whether you're selling yourself in a job
  interview, pitching a service or inspiring clients, the
  right story makes your message stick and helps people
  connect with you.

Stories for social media and podcasts

11

I did a bit of a LinkedIn experiment a few years ago. I was always sure that blogs including personal stories perform much better than content without a story. Over time, I noticed how they generate more likes, shares and comments, with people telling me how much they related to the stories.

So I started to experiment on my social media channels. I predominantly use LinkedIn but we also have Instagram and TikTok accounts for the Keeping it Real with Jac and Ral podcast.

When it comes to posting on LinkedIn, I know that it's not all about likes, shares and comments. But it is an excellent indication of whether your content is relevant, and this is the point of posting on LinkedIn. Your posts should be relevant, relatable and useful.

The results showed that my LinkedIn posts without a personal story received on average 3000 views. In contrast, my posts with personal stories received on average 30 000 views.

That's 10 times more traction. Ten times more effectiveness.

I have had a couple of posts sharing personal stories that have hit 50 000 or even 150 000 views.

One year, in honour of Mother's Day, I shared a story about my mum and the advice she gave me when I was 17. (I shared that story in chapter 6.) This post certainly struck a chord because it received over 2.5 million views, 24 000 reactions, 250 comments and 150 reposts.

I also noticed that when I shared clips on TikTok and Instagram from my podcast, it was always the clips of stories that received the most traction.

Don't be afraid to share personal stories on social media. Just make sure they are aligned with the personal brand you want to project and in the case of LinkedIn make sure they relate back to a business message. If you don't, you'll get all those keyboard warriors who have taken it upon themselves to be the LinkedIn police and inform you, 'This is not for LinkedIn'.

As I've mentioned, I run a podcast called Keeping it Real with Jac and Ral...I am the Ral of that duo, and we made a deliberate decision to share stories to bring our messages to life. So I want to kick off this section with the first story my co-host Jac Phillips shared on our very first podcast episode.

How do you know if you haven't tried?

Apart from being my podcast host, Jac Phillips also runs her own executive coaching business and sits on a variety of boards. I first met Jac in 2005 and she quickly became one of my favourite clients who then subsequently became one of my favourite friends.

Jac used to share the following story with her team and now she shares it with her coaching clients...and of course on our podcast.

The story

In my early 20s, I had a job as an on-air radio host in Perth. One day, the general manager walked into the studio and asked me if, as well as doing my on-air radio shift, I could also produce the commercials because we didn't have a producer. It was a fairly small radio station so we often took on several tasks.

He showed me the equipment used to do this producing and all I saw in front of me was a desk that looked like the cockpit of a plane. It was so bloody overwhelming...I had never seen anything like it before.

I can remember calling my dad and saying, 'Dad, I have been given this opportunity but I'm not sure if I can do it'. He said to me, 'Have you ever done it before?' and I said, 'No, that's the problem'. And to this day I remember his words, which were, 'If you have never done it before, how do you know you can't do it?'

So I gave it a go and of course, I could do it. Yes, I made some mistakes and I had to get people to show me a few things several times, but I could do it.

I have reminded myself of Dad's advice throughout my life: 'How do you know you can't do something if you haven't tried it before?'

Wise words from a wise man.

The result

Jac has shared the story on many different occasions to help people overcome their fears. She knows the story gives more gravitas to her advice of 'How do you know you can't do something if you haven't tried it before?' The story makes the message memorable.

Why it works

This showcases brilliantly that some of your most powerful stories happen when someone else is the hero. In this case, Jac's dad is the hero. The advice is coming from him. Jac is simply the conduit. (Well done, Merv.)

Luck in disguise

Brian Bacon is the founder and executive chair of the Oxford Leadership Group, which is a leading UK-based consultancy with more than one million international alumni. I came across Brian on LinkedIn when I read the following post. It resonated with me so much that I asked Brian if I could include it here.

The story

Winston Churchill once raised his glass and said, 'I prefer not to wish anyone health or wealth, but only luck. Because most people on the Titanic... were both healthy and rich. But very few of them were lucky'.

Did you know a senior executive survived the 9/11 attacks because he took his son to his first day of kindergarten?

Another man lived because it was his turn to grab doughnuts.

One woman survived because her alarm didn't go off.

Someone else was late because of a New Jersey traffic jam.

One person missed the bus.

Another spilled coffee and had to change clothes.

Someone's car wouldn't start.

Another returned home to answer a phone call.

One parent was delayed because their child was being unusually slow.

One man simply couldn't catch a cab.

But the story that struck me most? A man who wore new shoes to work that day. On his way, his feet hurt. He stopped at a pharmacy to buy bandaids. That's what saved his life.

Ever since I heard that, I think differently.

Now when I'm stuck in traffic...

When I miss the elevator...

When I forget something and have to turn back...

When my morning just doesn't go as planned...

I try to pause and trust:

- *Maybe this delay is not a setback.*
- *Maybe it's divine timing.*
- *Maybe I'm exactly where I'm meant to be.*

So next time your morning falls apart... the kids are slow, the keys go missing, you hit every red light... don't stress. Don't snap.

It might just be luck in disguise.

The result

The number of impressions, comments and reposts you get on a LinkedIn post is a brilliant indication of how it resonates. A quick look at Brian's previous 10 posts showed on average 59 impressions, four comments and nine reposts. This post had over 3070 impressions, over 250 comments and over 250 reposts. That's a great result.

Why it works

This is a great example of using micro stories to weave an overarching narrative. Starting with the quote from Winston Churchill to set the scene, Brian then lists all these micro stories ('…One woman survived because her alarm didn't go off…Someone's car wouldn't start…') and then brings it all back to his personal reflection and change of perspective of when things don't go to plan. Maybe it is luck in disguise.

Hot chocolate and workstations

Atul Sharma lives in Delhi, India and is a passionate trainer and facilitator. In 2014, he founded a learning space called Oasis of Learning. He believes in the power of stories and has shared many stories in his training sessions and on social media.

The following is one such story.

The story

Early in my career, I remember a specific day where I grabbed a hot chocolate and went back to my workstation. As I reached my workstation, my hand slipped and I ended up spilling my drink everywhere. My keyboard was covered in hot chocolate. I got a bit scared thinking that I would get in so much trouble off my boss for this.

I immediately called up IT for a replacement keyboard and then informed my boss about it. He didn't say anything to me.

The next day he came to our bay and told everyone to take a huddle break. He announced that he was running a 'Best Bay' contest and after a month the cleanest and most decorated bay would get a prize.

He appointed me as the bay manager for my bay and gave me 200 rupees. He told me, 'Atul, I trust you with this responsibility and I know you won't let me down'.

The next day I got some posters and balloons and decorated the bay. I also put some 'Keep your workstation clean' handouts at each team member's display board. After a month, the results were announced and our bay won the prize. He came over to me and patted my back. He handed over a coffee mug to me and said, 'For you to drink hot chocolate. Now, I can trust that you won't spill it' with a smile on his face.

This leadership behaviour of my boss stayed stamped in my mind. I learned that it is not important to talk about what went wrong. It is more important to give others an opportunity to correct their behaviour and create a suitable climate around it. On a personal level, I also learned that in case I make mistakes, I could correct them.

The result

Atul said the story has always been received very well. People share incidents from their lives where their managers were thoughtful and they also share incidents where the managers were not empathic. Atul says it makes him feel good that the story is able to highlight some essential qualities of an effective manager.

Why it works

It's another great example of a simple story used to deliver a powerful message. Your stories do not have to be about the major things in your life. Often these day-to-day, simple stories can be the most powerful.

Off tramping

I first met Ben Walker when I ran a thought leadership workshop in New Zealand and have been following his career with interest ever since. Ben often shares personal stories about his ultra-marathon running to communicate the messages of mindset. This is a story that he has shared on social media to communicate the right type of environment you need to push the boundaries and grow.

The story

On the weekend I took my two girls, Esmé and Eden, for a short hike and a night in a Central Otago back country hut.

For my 11-year-old, Eden, it was her first time staying in a Department of Conservation hut. She's not really into walking and her decision to come took more than a little thought.

I had both the girls pack up their own gear during the week. I had previously purchased both children kid-sized packs in the hope that we would get away hiking over the Christmas break. Unfortunately, due to the deluge of overseas visitors wanting to see New Zealand, we missed out on the famous 'Great Walks'.

The Boundary Creek Hut is considered a 'standard' hut, which means it has bunks with mattresses, a fire and a stream nearby for water. It's quite basic by most people's standards, but if you're equipped with the necessary kit then it's perfect.

With all of this in mind I wanted to make sure that I could assure my girls of some comfort outside their comfort zone. My goal was to make the trip enjoyable so that we could be assured of a trip number two.

I took a few steps to provide for a good experience:

1. Warm clothes, sleeping bag and jackets. Warm = happy.

2. *Dehydrated food of their choice. This was chicken carbonara, chocolate pudding and milos.*

3. *A safe experience that was achievable. The walk wasn't too far and the logistics were taken care of.*

The whole trip was a success. Esmé and Eden loved the whole time away and we're planning our next overnight excursion!

I'm sharing this story because I think it highlights the importance of providing a safe environment to push boundaries and grow. We now regularly go tramping and stay in huts. Each time there is at least one challenging aspect. The kids push through their perceived boundaries and grow as a result.

The result

Ben initially shared the story on LinkedIn and it was one of his better performing posts with lots of engagement and comments. Encouraged by that, he then started to share it to great effect in workshops with clients.

Why it works

This is another example of a simple personal story to communicate an important business message, in this case one that Ben is passionate about. The story is succinct with just the right amount of detail.

That's a wrap

- *Stories drive engagement on social platforms.* Posts with personal stories generally generate up to 10 times more views, reactions and comments than posts without stories, indicating that they are more relevant and relatable to audiences.

- *Stories make your personal brand memorable and meaningful.* As long as they align with your intended brand and connect back to a business or personal message, stories cut through the noise and can build trust.

- *Everyday moments can illustrate big lessons.* From luck and resilience to leadership and growth, small, personal anecdotes resonate more than grand or abstract claims.

- *Stories inspire interaction and reflection.* Whether in a podcast or LinkedIn post, stories invite audiences to see themselves in the message and spark comments, shares and discussion.

Stories around values

12

I believe there are two effective ways to demonstrate your values to others. The first is to actually live them. The second is to share stories about them.

I've been involved in my fair share of organisational values roll-outs, both when I worked in corporate and working alongside corporates to help them do just that. And I can say with authority that simply displaying your values on a wall, or a coffee mug, or on mousepads back in the day, never works. If only it were that simple.

To demonstrate your values (both at an individual level and an organisational level), you first need to be really clear on what those values mean to you. So, if you want to be known as collaborative or generous, then you need to be clear on what that means to you.

Once you have clarity, you'll be more consistent in your behaviour and actually live those values. Plus, you'll be better equipped to find an appropriate story that demonstrates that value.

I hope you find the following stories around values…well… of value.

Swim between the flags

Melissa Grasso was Head of Culture Development at a large financial institute where she was asked to present to her colleagues the plan to embed the company's values and behaviours into all their systems and processes.

The story

When I was 16, I was visiting my grandparents on the Gold Coast during the summer holidays. My sister and I often visited them over the summer, and we usually swam in their pool. But on this day I was out swimming in the surf. I was a very strong swimmer, having been swimming competitively for a number of years. But I wasn't familiar with swimming in the surf… and I certainly didn't know what a rip was. I did know that I was supposed to swim between the flags, but I didn't know that the flags were usually set up to keep people out of a rip.

So, I didn't really keep my eye on the flags.

And after a short while, I drifted outside the flags without knowing. Suddenly, I was caught in a rip.

I could feel straight away that I couldn't swim against the flow of the water and I was moving further and further away from the shore. But I didn't know you weren't supposed to swim straight for shore going directly against the flow of the rip.

I panicked.

I had never been so frightened in my life. So I swam hard and fast diagonally toward the shore. Eventually I made it back to shore utterly exhausted and relieved.

I was so grateful that I was such a strong swimmer and that I noticed the pull of the rip quickly. Later, I found out how many people drown in rips because they don't know to swim between the flags or how to get out of a rip. It was pure chance that I did this and I realised even more how truly lucky I was.

I'm sharing this with you because of the importance of keeping our eyes on the flags so we don't get caught in a rip. It reminds me of how important it is as an organisation to stay focused on our vision. To avoid drifting away from who we want to be.

For me, our organisation's purpose, vision, values and behaviours are like setting the flags in the sand. If we forget to keep our eyes on the flags, then we can easily drift away (without even noticing) from the core behaviours that we need to sustain to deliver exceptional service for our customers.

The result

Throughout the rest of the presentation, Melissa kept referring back to the flags as a metaphor. The feedback she received about the story on the day was really positive because it helped people connect with and understand her message.

What's more, she has had colleagues tell her that they keep thinking about the flags as a metaphor for the company's values and behaviours.

Why it works

Through this story, Melissa shows vulnerability by disclosing that she didn't know what to do and also uses language like 'I panicked' and 'I had never been so frightened in my life'. Sharing how you really felt helps people connect with your story. Swimming between the flags now becomes a metaphor for the organisation's purpose, vision and values. In the future, if people feel they are drifting from these values, they can remind each other by simply stating, 'We are drifting away from the flags' and people will be reminded of the story.

Right and fair

Dustin Bartley is Executive Manager in Workers Compensation for a large insurance company. I worked with Dustin a few years ago to help him find stories that would demonstrate to people why he is so passionate about doing what is right and fair.

Dustin had to speak to a group of more than 250 of his colleagues at a leadership event. He had a five-minute time allocation so we decided on sharing two stories about how he reacted in a moment of unfairness and the different ways he handled that. As Dustin had five minutes, he had time to combine two stories to illustrate how challenging it can be to do what is right and fair.

This is also a great example of sharing stories from one's youth, which is often when our values are formed.

The story

When I was four years old, I travelled with my parents to Seoul, South Korea, to adopt a five-month-old boy. He became my brother and my parents named him Blake.

Clearly Blake and I were physically very different. I became most aware of that not through the way he looked or behaved, because that became normal to me. I became aware of it through the way others treated him.

The hardest thing to contend with growing up with Blake was racism towards him. In the early 90s, Blake and I were at the public pool in Gilgandra, which is a small country town where my dad grew up.

I was 10 and Blake was six.

Most people in Gilgandra were either white Australians or of Indigenous background. While we were swimming, a group of kids my age started to pick on my little brother because he looked different. They called him 'Chinaman', imitated an accent, swore at him and bombed into the pool around us. It was intimidating and if it carried on, I knew Blake would be hurt.

I always wanted Blake to know that I had his back, no matter the situation, and I always wanted an outcome that was fair for everyone. In my mind, as a 10-year-old, that would have involved some sort of Jackie Chan routine that left the kids lying on the ground so Blake and I could swim and have an ice-cream. But that wasn't going to happen.

I asked the guys to quit it, which only made them more determined. So I had to make a decision. I took Blake to the other end of the pool, and they followed us. I then took him out of the pool and we went home.

I don't know if that was the right call, but it's the one I made. At that time, I knew that the values of care and justice were important to me. I didn't do a good job to protect Blake. I didn't get an outcome that was fair, and it hurt. I was ashamed and frustrated.

A year later, I found myself in a fight with a bully on the way home from school. His name was Daniel.

Daniel was bigger than me and he was picking on a guy from our grade and pushing him around.

As I walked past, I had a decision to make. I said to Daniel, 'Why don't you leave him alone; he's harmless'. He immediately came at me, yelled and tried to punch me in the face. Without thinking, I blocked it and punched him right in the jaw. He fell to the ground and then got up and ran home. Thank God, because I thought he would have belted me.

I expected to be in a whole lot of trouble.

The next day, however, the principal suspended Daniel. I wasn't suspended, and my dad took me out to KFC 'all you can eat'. I asked Dad, 'Why are we here?' He said to me, 'You shouldn't punch people, certainly not in the face, but if you are going to punch someone that's a good reason to do it'. It was nice to hear. My intention was to look out for others, and while I don't advocate for violence, I thought the outcome was important for everyone, including Daniel, and he wasn't such an ass when he got back to school.

For me, care and justice are at the core of being a good person and of good leadership. Growing up with Blake helped me realise that and my work experiences have reinforced it. I want to be known to stand for what's right and in a strange way I do look forward to the uncomfortable and character-building moments that come with that.

The result

Dustin first shared this story in 2022 and had shared the story again in various formats to reinforce the values that matter to him. He says, 'What I found the most surprising was the positive perception that complete strangers formed of me in that short, five-minute speech'.

'When I first shared it to 250 executives and senior leaders I really enjoyed having a very attentive crowd…seeing their smiles and in some instances tears but then hearing an overwhelming appreciation for the story and what it stood for.'

'That was almost three years ago and I still meet people today that thank me for sharing my story about Blake.'

Why it works

This is a great example of combining two stories to demonstrate how challenging this value can be. The first story is about a decision to protect his brother by leaving, while the second story is about standing up for and fighting… literally. The audience is left in no doubt about Dustin's strong values around fairness and standing up for what is right.

The story is quite emotive and can in some cases be triggering for people so mentioning that Dustin's dad took him out for KFC serves to lighten the story without detracting from its serious message.

Don't blame the bunny

Andrea Voigt is Group Head of Strategic Risk for a large organisation. I had the pleasure of mentoring Andrea when she was asked to give a short talk to over 300 leaders at a leadership conference.

She knew that her main message needed to be around the importance of taking accountability, especially in a leadership role.

We had a couple of mentoring sessions working on potential stories she could share and landed on 'Don't blame the bunny'.

The story

I grew up in South Africa and can distinctly recall a Nesquik TV commercial from the 80s that was of a little boy who would blame a bunny for drinking two glasses of Nesquik instead of one.

It is a saying that my parents would often say to me when I started making excuses for when things went wrong: 'Andrea, don't blame the bunny'.

My parents said it so often that I really thought it was a common, everyday saying. It wasn't until I was in my 40s that I found out it wasn't a common saying at all and it was only my family who said it.

It's a message we often hear as leaders: 'Take accountability and personal responsibility'. But let's be honest, always being accountable for everything that happens is hard.

This doesn't always come easily; sometimes it is much easier to 'blame the bunny'... also known as the 'system', the 'process' or (dare I say), someone else. It really is something we need to do consciously and deliberately.

Being prepared to challenge the status quo. Always asking, 'What could we do better? What can I/we improve? What can we learn from this and how can we move forward?' Or, when something does go wrong, asking ourselves, 'How did I contribute to this?' and 'What could I have done better?'

Just imagine what we could learn and achieve if we always looked for ways to improve... if we challenged the status quo, took accountability for what is within our control or influence and for decisions we make... instead of blaming the bunny!

The result

Andrea advised that she received great feedback from the story. She said, 'I personally rode that high for ages afterwards'. And that her team continued to reference 'Don't blame the bunny'.

She continues to use the story when asked to come and speak to other teams about her leadership values.

Andrea has since moved companies and now shares the story with her new team. She said that seeing the result of this story has encouraged her to think of other stories to make her messages stick.

Why it works

This is a fun story that includes a memorable tagline. As Andrea stated, her team continued to reference it. Stories like this with a simple tagline can become an easy way to call out behaviours.

Instead of having a difficult conversation with someone about not taking responsibility, it could be more easily addressed by saying 'Don't blame the bunny'.

Get married and have kids

Miranda Ratajski is Chief Information Officer of Group Business Units at Westpac, one of Australia's largest banks. She has been recognised in the Fintech Top 100 Women Globally, as an inclusive leader and included as a Woman of Influence by Women in Banking and Finance. She is also a part-time yoga teacher and is one of my many clients I now call a friend. If you picture what a typical CIO looks and acts like … Miranda is anything but that.

Miranda is a strong advocate for diversity in tech and first shared the following story in 2023 at the Tech Diversity Awards. It was recorded and is on YouTube. Here is an edited version.

The story

My mother left school when she was 12 years old. Her parents thought it was more important that her brothers have an education because she was only going to 'get married and have kids'. And this wasn't in a far-flung country … this was in Moonee Ponds, in Melbourne.

She put herself through night school, going on to work as a midwife. Now, for any of you who have had much to do with midwives, they say it as it is. Which makes complete sense: if you have a job where a bad shift can involve mothers or babies dying, you learn to put things into perspective, and I learned that at an early age.

Fast-forward a couple of years and I am 14 years old. A teenage daughter who knew everything, with a conservative father who knew he was always right. What could possibly go wrong?

Mum, Dad and I were sitting at the kitchen bench having a discussion about what I was going to study at university. Dad then calmly announced that there was no need for me to go to university as I was only going to get married and have kids. The aghast expression on my mum's face stays with me to this day.

Thanks to that 'gentle encouragement' by my dad, I had two undergraduate degrees and a Masters by the time I was 28 years old. But really that was all about Mum. She always told me I could be whatever I wanted to be, and I believed her. Play Aussie Rules? Of course I can. Work in technology even though I didn't study STEM and less than a third of the workforce were women? Of course I can do it. Work in financial services with lower ratios of women in leadership? Of course I can. Hell, why not do both!

So just like Mum, throughout my career I have used my privilege and position to promote inclusion and to attract more diversity into technology. My reasons for wanting more diversity are clear. There are some levels of altruism, but deep down, I want to win…and our chances of winning get better the more diversity and inclusion we have.

The result

Miranda uses the story to not only promote diversity but also courage and success. She says that people respond well to the core message of having the courage to do what is 'right for you', not necessarily what other people think is 'right for you'. People have strong reactions when you choose to go your own way despite lacking the full support of your family, though resilience enables you to persist on your chosen path.

Miranda told me that the 'you are just going to get married and have kids' comment always receives an extraordinarily strong response for a variety of reasons. She believes that what supports this story the most is hearing it from someone who doesn't look like most CIOs. From someone who did not take the 'normal route' and made it to being a CIO anyway.

Why it works

The story gives Miranda credibility around her messages of diversity. Through the story, you can see that this is not a recent passion for her or 'towing the organisation's values' but it really means something to her... and has ever since she was a teenager. There is also an appropriate use of humour used throughout the story, which is very much aligned to Miranda's style.

That's a wrap

- *Values are demonstrated through actions and stories, not slogans.* Simply displaying values on walls or mugs is meaningless unless people live them and share stories that illustrate them.

- *Stories bring clarity and consistency to values.* Being clear on what your values mean to you enables you to behave consistently and find meaningful stories to demonstrate your values.

- *Personal, vulnerable stories resonate deeply.* Stories of struggle, growth or lessons learned (such as swimming in a rip, standing up for someone or challenging expectations) humanise values and make them relatable.

- *Stories with a memorable metaphorical tagline can continue to reinforce the message.* Phrases like 'Swim between the flags' and 'Don't blame the bunny' become shorthand for maintaining focus and accountability within teams.

- *Stories that align with lived experience build credibility and connection.* Whether advocating for diversity, fairness or inclusion, stories grounded in personal history show authenticity and inspire others to embrace the same values.

Stories for influence, change and inspiration

13

A long time ago, I was working in a senior change management role and implementing a major technology change across an entire organisation of 25 000 employees.

As a change manager, one of my jobs was to work with the business units and department heads to help them implement the change. Of course, with any change you are often met with resistance...and rightly so because change is disruptive. And this one was going to be significantly disruptive to the way they currently worked.

What I found, however, is that when I shared a story in these presentations about why the change was coming, and the benefits to acknowledging the disruption, I noticed it seemed to get the message across better. People didn't appear to be so quick to defend the status quo. There seemed to be a greater acknowledgement of the change being needed and it made the next steps a little easier on everyone.

It wasn't a silver bullet and didn't remove all the challenges, but I would often notice a positive shift in the way people responded to the messages of change.

Stories are a critical communication tool when it comes to inspiring people to act. Here are a few examples of stories people have shared to influence others.

FBI special switchboard agent

I first met Dr Rhonda Glover Reese at Harvard in 2016, and a few years later, she attended some of my training seminars in New York. She is my favourite FBI agent (granted, she is the only FBI agent I have met).

Rhonda has since retired from the FBI and is now CEO of the Rhonda M Glover Group, which is a coaching and leadership development firm dedicated to people's growth, personal and professional development, and transformation.

She is also a certified professional coach with a niche in career coaching focusing on law enforcement personnel and those interested in law enforcement as a career.

She shares the following story at conferences, workshops, leadership seminars or in coaching sessions, as well as in her recently published book *Ascending to Leadership: Strategies I learned from more than 30 years as an FBI agent*.

The story

When I was a little girl, I would religiously watch The FBI with Efrem Zimbalist Jr. What is really funny about that is I would watch the show every day except Sunday, but I only remember one episode. It was about a little girl who had been kidnapped and the kidnappers kept her in a box buried underground with a straw. *That is how I remembered it. Whether or not that episode happened that way, this is my story and I'm sticking to it.*

Fast-forward to 10th grade in high school. I was in my guidance counsellor's office and there I noticed a pamphlet on a bookrack. I pointed to it and said in my head, 'That's it! I am going to be a Special Agent with the FBI!' I did not waiver, I did not move, I was unapologetic in my determination. I was going to be an FBI Special Agent.

After graduating from college, I applied to the FBI in a support position. I could either be a clerk or a clerk typist. Since I did not pass the typing test, I was offered a position as a clerk.

I reported for duty at FBI Headquarters and was so excited about working at the FBI. I did not know what I would be doing but I was working at the FBI. I was escorted to the Flag Room, which is now known as the Webster Room, for a three-day orientation still not knowing where I would be assigned.

Throughout the orientation there were side conversations about people not wanting to be assigned to Division 1 (Identification Division) or Division 3 (Records Management). It was all about production in those divisions, and lacked growth potential. On the third day of orientation, I was told I would be going to Division 8, Technical Services. Someone told me the computers were in this division and it was a good assignment. I was so excited, more so because I was not going to Division 1 or 3.

A woman came to the Flag Room to escort me to where I would be working. She was quite fabulous for that time. She had poufy hair, her make-up was impeccable, she had on a poufy skirt and wore cat glasses. She took me into a small conference room and welcomed me to the FBI. She then proceeded to tell me that I was assigned to the FBI switchboard as telephone operator. I said, 'The switchboard?' She responded with, 'No-one told you?' I said, 'No'.

She was so sweet. She apologised because she saw how distraught I had become. So many things were running through my head…what are my friends going to say? What about my family? I can't tell anyone I am working on the switchboard. I have a college degree. Surely this must be a mistake.

As I fought back tears, the woman escorted me to an area in the switchboard room where calls were coming in from all over the country and the world seeking information.

That area of the room was called 'Information'. I took a minute to call my mother as I continued to fight back the tears. I told Mum that I was assigned as a telephone operator. She proceeded to say, 'Well, I guess someone heard your voice and thought you would be good on the switchboard'.

At that moment there was a shift in my mindset. From that day forward, I decided I was going to learn everything I could about the FBI switchboard. I volunteered for different shifts, took on assignments and learned as much as I could about the switchboard. I started to meet people at different levels within the FBI. I talked to the director and other FBI executives on a daily basis, and in the process, became really good friends with some high-ranking bureau officials. I quickly learned that the switchboard was the zenith of activity. Everything came through the switchboard.

After my mother's comment, it was like a switch came on in my head. Because I showed up differently, my attitude changed, I showed up in excellence, I stepped up and doors started to open. Opportunities started to chase me down.

I am here to tell you that you may have switchboard moments where you will have to ask yourself, 'How can I use this experience to get me to where I want to be? What do I need to do with this?' Well, you need to get ready to be ready so opportunities can chase you down. Show up in excellence and do your best in everything that you do. You don't know who is watching you and considering you for that next position or promotion. Don't worry about that. Position yourself and do your best and it will happen!

The result

Rhonda says that when she shares the story she is very intentional about being descriptive. She says, 'I want everyone to understand what I was feeling. I want people to walk my journey with me. It was key that people understood how I almost derailed my employment with the FBI. That my childhood dream was to become an FBI agent, but I was about to commit self-sabotage with my faulty mindset'.

Rhonda says that this story is very effective in giving space to people needing to experience a shift in their mindset and that she will continue to share it.

Why it works

I first heard this story from Rhonda when she ran it past me for feedback in a restaurant in Washington DC. I loved it immediately for several reasons, including the humility she showed in being devastated that her big FBI career was starting as a telephone operator. The story also works because even though it was Rhonda who embraced this, it was the comment her mother made that was the catalyst.

Jiggle the lock

I first met Pia Silva when she attended a storytelling workshop I ran in New York in 2024. Pia was facilitating a retreat the following week for the small agency owners she coaches and this is the story she shared.

The story

Back in 2009, my partner and I were living just a few blocks away, barely scraping by. We were doing catering, gig work, freelancing … whatever we could to make ends meet. One of the ways we brought in extra money was by renting out apartments upstairs on Airbnb.

Over time, I started noticing a pattern. Every month, dozens of guests would check in, all following the same instructions to unlock the door.

Eighty per cent of people had no problem. They followed the instructions, found the key box, turned the key and got inside.

Another 10 to 15 per cent struggled at first. They would text me, saying the key wasn't working, and I'd tell them, 'I promise it works. It's just a little sticky. Keep trying'. And sure enough, they'd jiggle the key a little more and the door would open.

Then there was the 5 per cent. No matter what I told them, they refused to believe the lock worked. They insisted it was broken and would not keep trying. The only way they were getting inside was if I showed up in person and opened the door for them.

I started to realise, there are two kinds of people in this world. Some will take the key and jiggle the lock until it opens. They'll persist. They'll trust that it works, even when it takes longer than expected. And then there are others who, the moment they hit resistance, decide the lock is broken and give up.

I'm sharing this because it reminds me of how different people tackle the work we do on these retreats. Some of you will take the key we give you, put it in the lock and jiggle it until the door opens — unlocking a completely new and exciting space. Others will jiggle the key a few times, get frustrated, and decide the hallway's good enough. Or you'll assume the lock is broken and the key doesn't work. But here's the truth: no matter where you are in your business, there's always a door waiting to be opened. You may not even know the space exists yet, but it's there — and it's valuable. You just have to be willing to keep jiggling the lock until it opens.

The result

Pia reported back to me that throughout the entire retreat people were talking about jiggling their lock and it became a mantra of the retreat. One person even got a key tattoo at a local parlour before the event ended!

Can you believe that? I couldn't. I had to go back and clarify with Pia that she was talking about a real tattoo. She was. So, if you ever doubted that stories can have a permanent and long-lasting impact, doubt no more. Because there are very few things that are more permanent and long lasting than a tattoo!

Why it works

This is such a simple, visual story that it does not surprise me someone got a tattoo after hearing it...okay, that does surprise me a bit and I am a bit jealous as I'm not sure anyone has got a tattoo after hearing any of my stories. Jiggling the lock becomes a strong metaphor she can use with her clients to help them unlock business success.

Kissing frogs

This story comes from Penelope Barr, who runs her own coaching company helping people and organisations transition from where they are to where they want to be. Because Penelope is all about helping people deal with change, this is a story Penelope shares in a variety of scenarios.

The story

I'd kissed a lot of frogs in my dating life. And I decided it was time.

Time to find that match.

People always told me love comes along when you least expect it. That's never been my experience. But I finally felt ready to find someone, get married and have a child. I knew I needed to do this my way. So I thought about what's worked for me in the past, and what I really wanted. I made a list. Not any old list but a prioritised, weighted list.

I then set about on my travels. I was being posted to a few countries for work, to roll out what I'd created in Australia. A perfect opportunity to test my list. The frog-sifting continued. I shared my list with everyone I met. I was all in. Nearly two years later, lots of fun times but no promise of lifelong times.

And then, I saw him.

Through a window, jauntily walking along. He joined our table and we spoke. Much later, over drinks, he lamented about the fact I was going back to Australia, because we'd been having such a great time.

I told him I was going home to get married and have a child. Oh! He was surprised because I hadn't mentioned a fiancé. I explained. I'm going home to find a husband and we will have a child. I then shared my list with him.

He said, 'Wow, the person you tell is going to have to be sorted to hear this'.

He realised soon after he was that person.

I share this story because nothing can get in the way of a strong vision, a clear plan, the support of others and optimising every opportunity. Create a plan and go for it.

The result

Penelope says this story is very effective to share with anyone looking for a partner, a new job or a new house. You only need one of anything.

Why it works

I love the start of this story as it really hooks you in. I also like how the story is about finding romantic love but adopting a business approach of the weighted and prioritised list to do that. And it's perfectly linked at the end to the message of having a vision and a plan.

That's a wrap

- *Stories shift mindsets and reduce resistance to change.* Sharing relatable stories during change initiatives helps people understand the reasons behind the change, making them more open and engaged.

- *Personal and vulnerable stories inspire action.* Whether it's an FBI agent starting on a switchboard, a facilitator persevering through resistance or a coach finding love with a plan, authentic stories connect emotionally and motivate others.

- *Stories create memorable metaphors and mantras.* Phrases such as 'Jiggle the lock' and 'kissing frogs' can become symbolic reminders for persistence and planning.

- *Simple, visual stories stick and spread.* Stories told well (like the Airbnb lock metaphor) resonate deeply, sometimes even inspiring long-term personal symbols like tattoos or becoming involved in team culture.

Stories for coaching or life advice 14

I truly believe that experience is the best teacher, but storytelling can be just as good. A great story can teach somebody something without them having to experience the pain that sometimes goes with it.

We share stories to protect our children from harm. We want to teach them about harmful things without the need for them to actually experience the harm. Sometimes we share stories to pass on wisdom or to inspire.

Take this one for instance (this is also a great example of how you can share a parable with a personal touch).

Recently, I was walking along the beach with my daughter Alex and we were having a philosophical conversation about higher purpose and making a difference. Maybe it was because we were walking along the beach, but it reminded me of a parable that I shared with her:

'A man was walking along a beach littered with thousands of starfish, all stranded under the scorching sun. As he walked, he gently picked up one starfish at a time and threw them back into the ocean, saving each one from certain death.

After a while, a fisherman watching from nearby called out, "What are you doing? There are too many starfish. You'll never make a difference".

The man paused, picked up another starfish, and tossed it into the water. Then he turned and said, "I made a difference to that one".'

Sometimes making a difference feels like it has to be tied to a grand mission or a higher calling. But more often, it's about the small, intentional actions we take each day. The moments where we show up, connect and care for just one person.

So, let me ask you ... Who is your starfish today?

Whether it is providing coaching for one of your team or helping a friend or colleague work through a challenge or a teaching moment with your child or student, a story can often be the most effective thing to share.

The power of authentically showing up

Kavita Lobo is a leadership coach from Mumbai, India who often uses stories to get her messages across. The following story is one she shares about showing up authentically.

The story

It was a high-energy session, one of those moments where everything clicks. I had just finished delivering my presentation to a room of over 200 people. Together, we had moved, reflected, laughed and explored questions like, 'What and who gives you joy?'

I was on a high, not just from the energy in the room, but from the satisfaction that comes when you know you've created meaningful impact.

Later that evening, there was a party…music, lights and conversations buzzing in every corner. It was expected that I'd continue riding that energy wave…mingling, laughing and being part of the crowd.

But instead, I felt…lost.

I stood there, surrounded by cheerful faces and lively chatter, yet feeling completely disconnected. I couldn't quite place it, but I knew this feeling. It's happened before.

So, I quietly stepped away, deciding to walk back to my room instead.

On my way back, I asked myself, Why do I do this? Why does this happen so often?

And then it struck me…this is me.

I realised that while I can show up fully in a room packed with people, holding space for meaningful conversations, I'm not someone who thrives in social situations that feel surface-level. I've learned that I'm more comfortable in quieter spaces, in one-on-one conversations where depth takes over.

I show up when it matters…when I feel I can contribute meaningfully. And when my role is done, I'm content to step away, not because I don't belong, but because I know where I am my most authentic self.

That evening taught me something important: that being an introvert doesn't make me any less impactful. It doesn't take away from the energy I bring when I stand in front of a room full of people. It simply means I recharge differently.

And I'm okay with that.

For me, knowing how we show up is just as important as when we show up and that presence isn't about being everywhere... it's about showing up in the moments that matter most.

The result

Kavita has shared this story in her coaching and facilitation sessions, where it has had a profound impact on participants. They have been able to relate to the story, learn from it and reflect on their own experiences. She has also shared it on other platforms, including LinkedIn, and advised that she received many personal messages from people for whom the story resonated and who shared their own similar experiences.

Why it works

The story reveals vulnerability and confidence at the same time and is a story that many people could relate to. You can visualise and feel the pain of Kavita as she walks back to her room, beating herself up, and then the relief when she accepts that what she has done is totally okay.

You can cross now

I first met Dan Stubbs when he attended one of my storytelling workshops. So impressed I was of his leadership, I asked him to be a guest on my now-finished podcast, Authentic Leadership.

Dan is legally blind and is the Commissioner at the Victorian Disability Worker Commission. He often shares this story in a variety of situations.

The story

Once, I was standing on the corner of Bourke and King Streets, waiting to cross at the lights but also checking my text messages as I knew that the friend I was meeting at the café across the road would text me that they are running late.

And I am blind so I was listening to my text messages via an air pod and with my white cane in my other hand.

The text that I was receiving seemed to be saying that my friend was suggesting we meet somewhere else so I was listening to the text message again and the lights went green.

Then, imagine my shock and feeling of disorientation when someone grabbed me to take me across the road because they assumed I needed help to do that! They didn't ask me anything. They told me (like you would tell a child), 'You can cross now but be quick as there's a tram coming'. I know there was good intention there, but I had crossed that road hundreds of times before and didn't need help…

I'm sharing this with you because people always want to know what is the best way to help, or offer to help, a person with a disability.

I want everyone to remember that they need to stop themselves from 'helping' and, instead, put the person with a disability in the driver's seat. Putting the person with a disability in charge is empowering them to tell you what they need.

If I, as a person with a disability, perceive that you are just going to help me based on your own assumptions and preconceptions, I am most likely not going to accept your offer of help … even if I actually need it.

So I invite you to help people with a disability, but ask them first if they need your help.

The result

Dan has found that sharing examples of his own lived experience helps him communicate his messages with greater impact.

Why it works

When you hear this story, it makes you reflect on what you have done or what you would do in this situation. Well, that certainly happened when Dan shared the story with me. The story has greater impact than simply telling people what they should or should not do.

Trust your intuition

Debbie Twiss works in the dairy industry and shares the following story at training events to encourage people to trust their intuition.

The story

During a lull in conversation at my husband's religious family Christmas gathering, my husband pipes up with, 'Debbie knows a joke…' I am a dairy cattle veterinarian and the only joke I had told my husband recently was down at the cattle yards while castrating a bull, and I was pretty sure that this was not the occasion to share said joke.

I'm relieved when my father-in-law starts telling more stories and I mentally wipe sweat off my brow.

Five minutes later, with lunch still cooking in the oven and my father-in-law out of steam, my husband takes the opportunity to again promote my joke-telling. I consider the situation, decide that my husband knows his family better than me and share this joke:

'Horse and chicken are great mates but not the brightest crayons in the box. While out walking in the forest, Horse falls in a horse-sized quicksand hole and starts sinking quickly. He calls to his mate Chicken, "Help, help, I'm going to die".

'Chicken says, "Don't worry, Horse, I'll save you". Chicken races off and comes back driving a Mercedes. Chicken ties a rope on the Mercedes tow ball and throws the other end to Horse saying, "Grab onto the rope and I'll pull you to safety!" Horse grabs on and Chicken pulls him to safety. Horse is grateful and promises to be there for Chicken if he is ever in trouble.

'A week later, Horse and Chicken are out for a walk again and Chicken falls into a chicken-sized quicksand hole and started sinking quickly. He calls to his mate Horse, "Help, help, I'm going to die."

'Horse says, "Don't worry Chicken, you were there for me last week. I'll save you. Now, Chicken, I'm going to stand over this quicksand hole, and I'll let down my old boy. You grab on and I'll pull you to safety". That is precisely what Horse did, and Chicken was saved.

'The moral of the story is that if you are hung like a horse, you do not need a Mercedes to pick up chicks.'

The moment I deliver the punchline, the atmosphere of the room crashes like the proverbial train wreck. There is shocked silence except for my father-in-law choking in the corner barely managing to stifle a fit of giggles.

The icing on the cake of my fall from family grace was my husband's horrified expression and gasp of, 'Debbie, how could you say that joke?'

After lunch I pulled my husband aside and asked WTF at being thrown under the bus. To which my husband, who was now being regarded as some sort of saint by his mother for the wife he had to bear, nonchalantly replied, 'I didn't remember the punchline'.

I did remember the punchline, and my instinct told me I shouldn't share the joke. I should have trusted my instinct.

The result

Debbie said the story worked really well to set up the context of the training and said many people still remember the story. Debbie still does cattle work, but informed me that she no longer tells her husband jokes.

Why it works

I love the visuals in this story. Not only the visuals in the joke but the visuals of Debbie being hesitant to share the joke. Then the reaction of her family, and then pulling her husband aside.

That's a wrap

- *Stories teach without the pain of direct experience.* Like parables and personal anecdotes, stories can impart wisdom, protect from harm and inspire action in a way that sticks.

- *Stories help people see value in small, meaningful actions.* The starfish parable reminds us that making a difference doesn't always require grand gestures; it's about helping one person at a time.

- *Personal vulnerability makes stories relatable.* From Kavita accepting her introversion to Dan advocating for how to help people with disabilities, sharing honest stories fosters empathy and reflection.

- *Stories inspire self-awareness and authenticity.* Whether it's trusting your instincts, showing up where it matters or empowering others to direct their own help, stories invite introspection and growth.

- *Humour and humility enhance connection.* Lighthearted yet meaningful stories (like Debbie's joke gone wrong) demonstrate that even mistakes can teach powerful lessons when told authentically.

Stories for speeches and eulogies 15

There will most likely be times in your life when you need to deliver a speech. That could be at your best friend's wedding or your child's 21st birthday. It could be when you are asked to deliver a eulogy or a farewell to an employee.

There have been many times during my storytelling workshops when I have had participants tell me they want to totally rewrite a speech. One was a best-man speech at his best friend's wedding, and another I recall was a man delivering a speech at his daughter's wedding.

It's a good idea to practise the speech out loud several times, as the first few times you share these stories they can be quite emotional.

This section includes two of my stories.

Release Russell

Back in 2001, my best friend Gail got married and I made a speech. It was probably one of the best speeches I have made. The guests loved it and everyone was in hysterics laughing. The reason it was so impactful was because I included one specific story. The following is my entire speech, which is basically one story. Well, a story within a story.

The story

I have always wanted to say a speech at Gail's wedding and I thank Gail and Russell for the opportunity to do so. My reason is purely selfish in that I have a plethora of embarrassing stories about Gail that I would so much love to share with you all. But seeing how this is a special day for Gail and Russell, I will save those for Gail's 40th or 50th birthday.

So in thinking of what I could say in my speech tonight, I remembered how I knew Gail's relationship with Russell was serious because she never had a nickname for him.

Let me explain...

Gail and her friend Jo (not me, because I was far too mature) would always come up with some name for any boy they liked or who liked them... Men were just one big game to those two girls.

Gail would have names for her dates, such as:

- *Spider: something to do with the shape of the guy's legs.*

- *Perfect Pete: because he had to have everything perfect.*

- *Paxton Pete: because his ex was going out with the father of those Paxton losers.*

When she ran out of names, she would just revert to Steve 1 and Steve 2, and when she and Jo could not think of anything, they would come up with names like Jelly Bean... because they were eating jelly beans at the time of trying to think of a name for the poor unfortunate soul.

One was even called Safety Pin, but that's a story for another time...you'll have to come to her 40th to hear that one.

The fact that Russell never had a name meant that Gail might have been taking this relationship seriously. I conveyed my thoughts to Jo when I was told that Russell did in fact have a name and his name was Release.

And the story goes like this...

Gail, Jo and a group of single friends would go to the Beaconsfield Hotel on a Sunday night to check out the male talent. If one of the girls liked a boy, they would place a hold on him, which meant the others could not attempt to chat him up in any way (I told you men were just a game to them).

Gail, of course, being besotted by Russell's striking good looks, sophisticated dress sense and charm, put a hold on him. She then proceeded to place holds on several other boys throughout the night. The other girls...being fed up with Gail placing holds on every Tom, Dick and Harry that walked by...made up a new rule: you were only allowed to have three holds at any one time.

Gail, who currently had four holds, was forced to release one of her holds. After weighing up the pros and cons of every hold she had, she cried out, 'Release Russell!'

And hence he was called Release from then on...

Needless to say, she eventually came to her senses and put a hold back on Russell.

So I would just like to wish Gail and Russell all the very best for their married life together. And I am so glad, as I am sure everyone here is, that tonight they have both placed permanent holds on each other, never to be released.

The result

The number of comments I received on the night saying that was the best wedding speech was testament to the power of one short story. Twenty-four years on, I still have some people comment on it. By the way, Gail and Russell still have a permanent hold on each other (although they have just purchased a caravan, so that might be tested).

Why it works

The story works because it focuses on a funny story that provides an insight into Gail that many in the audience did not know. It was short and entertaining in an environment where many wedding speeches go on for way too long.

Should have gone for it

Jonathan Wray lives in Canada and shared the following story at his friend's wedding, where he was best man to the groom, Fred.

The story

Fred and I spent a lot of time in cars as teenagers. He would often drive me to youth group meetings in his family's Chevette, and we also completed driving school together.

Fred was a pretty good driver. I never felt that I was in any particular danger when Fred was driving. But Fred had one annoying tendency while driving. He would often hesitate on his left-hand turns, uncertain whether he had enough time and space to safely turn ahead of the approaching cars. He would inevitably wait too long and miss the opportunity to turn and then have to wait longer for the next opportunity to turn. Every time this happened (and it happened a lot), Fred would say, 'Darn, I should have gone for it'.

Well, I'm glad to say that we won't hear those words today. Thankfully, Fred took the opportunity to ask Donna out on that first date, and eventually to ask her to marry him. He didn't wait too long and miss out on this wonderful opportunity. He didn't have to say, 'Darn, I should have gone for it'.

Fred, all of us gathered here today are happy to know you didn't hesitate, that you went for it and asked Donna to be your bride. We wish you a life full of happiness together. But if I could give you one piece of advice when you are out driving with Donna: try to avoid those left-hand turns ... or better yet, let Donna drive!

The result

Jonathan said the story worked out well and that he got lots of laughs during the speech and positive comments about the speech after the wedding ceremony.

Why it works

I love how this story gives an insight to his friend Fred. It's a short and funny story ... a great way to show how glad he was that Fred didn't hesitate in asking Donna to be his bride, honouring both groom and bride.

My dad's eulogy

I have delivered hundreds of professional speeches over my career, but the most important speech I delivered was the eulogy for my father in 2019. I spent a lot of time preparing for it due to its significance.

I knew the priest would be doing the usual timeline speech for Dad. Where he was born, where he grew up, the jobs he had, the children he had, and so on. Priests can do a timeline speech because they usually don't know the person, or don't know them very well. They are simply stating facts.

I wanted my eulogy to be more heartfelt...to highlight Dad's values. But instead of just stating them, I wanted to share specific stories.

I debated whether to include something as personal as Dad's eulogy in this book. I also thought it might be too long for people to read and thought an edited version would be better. In the end, I decided to include it in its entirety for three reasons.

The first and main reason is that I do think it showcases the process of being clear on the messages you want to convey and then using a selection of short stories to do that.

The second reason, and perhaps this is a bit self-indulgent, is that it provides an opportunity to capture Dad's life in print and let his light and legacy spread a little further.

The final reason is to test, and hopefully show you, the power of stories for creating real connections.

I encourage you to read about a man you don't know and will never meet. As you read this, take notice of your emotions. And ask yourself:

- Are you feeling you are starting to get to know this man?

- Are you feeling a bit of a connection?

- Would you have liked to meet him?

If you answered yes, I can guarantee you're feeling that way because of the stories I share about him.

The story

About 10 years ago, for Mum's 75th birthday, the entire family had a weekend away up at Yarrawonga, a place we spent every Christmas for well over 20 years.

At night, we were all sitting around the campfire and when Dad looked around at all his children and grandchildren, he said, 'I started all this'. And that he did … granted Mum had a fair bit to do with it also.

Mum and Dad met when they were 18 and 19 respectively and married a few years later. In January, they would have celebrated their 65th wedding anniversary.

Mum and Dad had eight children, 14 grandchildren and seven great-grandchildren, with no doubt more to come.

Dad was born in Coldstream in 1932, spending the majority of his youth in Bright. And if you are ever in Bright and go to the Garden Gallery café, that is Dad's old home. He was the youngest of three children, being the baby brother to his sister Georgia and brother Hopetoun.

And while Georgia lived in Myrtleford, Dad and Uncle Hopetoun were literally inseparable growing up, living in the same street for almost their entire adult lives. We holidayed together, we lived across the road from each other in Reservoir and when we moved to Greensborough both families moved and lived in the same street two doors away from each other. When Uncle Hopetoun passed away and Mum and Dad moved to a unit in Diamond Creek, Dad made sure Aunty Elaine came with them. So now they live next door to each other.

Prior to all that, Dad's family moved to Thornbury when Dad was a young teenager and at age 14 he started working for a furniture company where he was a French polisher for over 20 years. Dad's other occupation was as a spray painter, which he did for about another 20 years before retiring at 59 due to ill health. But, as I'm sure you all know, that was never going to stop him from working. He resumed his love of French polishing, doing jobs for family and friends, with some people here today being the recipients of Dad's skill and craft.

Dad went by a variety of names…

His official name was Haydn John MacFarlane Gregory Chapman… don't you love a five-name name?

He was H to his workmates.

Uncle H to his nephews.

Old Boy to some.

And of course, Dad and Pa.

He also had a bit of a nickname and that was Lazarus, earned because of the number of times he defied death.

At age 46, Dad had a massive heart attack and the doctors told Mum he would not live through the night… not something you want to hear with eight young children.

When he was about age 67 we were all called to emergency late on a Saturday night because we were again told he would not make it through the night. By the time we got there he was sitting up in bed, so we ordered pizza and ate it in the emergency ward. There were so many of us that we may or may not at some stage have been asked to keep the noise level down or leave.

The doctors had told Dad he would not live a day past 70 and on his 70th birthday he woke and proudly declared that they got that wrong. Think of the additional experiences Dad *had in those extra 17 years, including, more recently, two Richmond premierships. And for all the Richmond supporters here, I wouldn't be expecting any more flags in the near future because believe me, if it was going to happen, Dad would still be hanging in here.*

As Dad's health deteriorated over the last few years, he still kept defying the time frames that the doctors gave us. We assumed it would always be the last Christmas, last Father's Day, last birthday … but he always made it to the next one.

Six weeks ago, they turned off Dad's defibrillator in his pacemaker and we were again told that the end would come pretty quickly, but his heart never failed him.

When Dad went into palliative care, they suggested he would only have one or two days to live, but he hung in for eight days.

A fighting spirit and positive mindset were two amazing attributes of Dad's, but he had others.

Mainly, he was an ideas man. Dad was always figuring out a quicker way to do something or to make things better.

His grandmother once said to him, 'One of these days, Haydn, you are going to invent something that will change the world'.

For example, well before we had heard of Kärchers, Dad got a broom, drilled a hole in the head and attached a hose to it so he could clean the windows and the cars with the broom and have a constant flow of water to it.

Well before we ever saw aerating shoes for the lawn, Dad had a block of wood with nails in it that he would strap to his feet and aerate the lawn with.

A lot of his sentences would start with, 'I've been thinking, it would be better if …'

If there was a way to do it better, Dad would find it and if not, he would give it a go. In his last months, he was even tinkering with his medication, ignoring the expert advice of the leading heart and kidney specialist in the country.

Dad didn't really have any hobbies because he spent his life in service to others. He was always building things, fixing things or improving things. This included not only his own house but those of his children, grandchildren and friends.

Almost everything was built, not bought. Growing up, Dad built every piece of play equipment we had in the backyard (which was a lot). He built:

- *house extensions*

- *sheds*

- *cubby houses*

- *our swimming pool, which had a tap at the bottom to drain the water*

- *a billiards table, which always had a bit of a lean in one corner*

- *a table tennis table*

- *skateboards*

- *billy carts (we even had one that was a replica of the Fred Flintstone car)*

- *skiffle boards.*

When tread shoes were in fashion in the 70s, Dad would add old car tyres to shoes. Glad I missed that fashion statement.

When Lazy Susans were all the rage, he built those, which we thought were pretty cool.

When the bike of choice was dragsters, Dad changed all the handlebars and converted all our bikes to dragsters.

Shane (my brother) can even recall Dad making a cannon and using a beer can with a firecracker in it as the cannonball. Fortunately, that didn't work, so he resorted to pinning firecrackers to the clothes line and spinning them around.

About 10 years ago, Dad helped Steve (my husband) build a new back wall at our place and when I questioned how strong it would be Dad replied with, 'That is as strong as the bloody Great Wall of China and is not falling down'. Then he added, 'And if it does, I won't be around to fix it'.

In true Lazarus style, that Great Wall of China started falling down a few years ago.

Dad was ultimately a teacher. He taught us to do everything and to never discriminate based on us being girls or boys. He taught us how to paint, how to change our tyres, basic car maintenance, how to use a drill, how to use a soldering iron, a pot rivet gun and so much more.

He had a tremendous amount of confidence in our capabilities…sometimes way too much. And this, combined with his disregard for any health and safety standards (that was a sign of the times) meant it was amazing we…and he, for that matter…survived.

I can still recall Dad fixing something electrical in the roof. My job was to turn the electricity mains off while he worked on it and back on for him to test it. 'On, off, on, off,' were the calls from the roof until I heard Dad scream and then yell, 'Who bloody turned the electricity back on?' To this day I am convinced he said 'on'.

Another example of OH&S not being high on Dad's agenda was around the use of ladders. He never really took much notice of 'Don't stand on the top rung'. Maybe it was out of necessity because he was so short, but he was once on a ladder drilling on the roof when we heard him yelling out for help. We all ran outside to see that he had fallen off the ladder but was hanging onto the guttering while the drill was still spinning around. It was caught in his sock and Dad was yelling, 'Turn the bloody drill off and get the ladder'. (Dad said bloody a lot.)

These incidents never deterred him though.

Dad was easy-go-lucky, with a real 'She'll be right mate' positive attitude. As a classic example of this, four days before his death, while he was in palliative care, we went to visit him and he turned to Jess and said, 'How ya going, love?' and Jess said, 'Pretty good, Pa. How are you?' To which he replied, 'Not bad'. Jess has now decided she wants a tattoo that says 'How ya going, love?' But I think she thinks that might be the only way to get a tattoo and not get in trouble off Nana.

Dad called most people 'love' or 'mate'... again, pure process improvement as he would say... you never get anyone's name wrong if they are all 'love' or 'mate'.

And from where I stand, I can see many of those loves and mates here today.

I think a sign of how loyal Dad was is reflected in his friendships, which are longstanding. And although most of his male friends are no longer with us (not that it's a competition, but Dad did outlast nearly everyone), their families are.

Dad and Rollo Jackson first met when they were about 15 playing football together, and Mum and Dad and Kath and Rollo were lifelong friends. Kath and Rollo had eight kids also (all are here today) and every five weeks we would go to their house or they would come to ours. No doubt Rollo and Dad are reminiscing about those days now.

On behalf of my family, I would like to thank you for all attending and, let's face it, when your funeral is at full capacity with standing room only, it's a sign of being well loved and touching a lot of people.

We would also like to thank Dad's doctors and carers who helped him over the years.

A special thanks to Lynne and Leeanne, who shouldered the bulk of looking after Dad these last few years, taking him to hospital and doctors' appointments and helping Mum.

And to Mum, who successfully managed to keep Dad out of aged care. You truly personified your wedding vows of 'in sickness and in health' and 'until death us do part'.

Finally, I just want to say if anyone could write an instruction manual on how to live a good life, it would be Haydn Chapman. There would be a section on:

- *How to serve others*
- *How to have a positive mindset*
- *How to put things in perspective*
- *How to not take things seriously.*

There would probably also be a section on how Builders Bog or WD40 could fix almost anything.

I reckon a lot of people would read this instruction manual on how to live a good life. Except I know of one person who never would. Dad. Because ironically, Dad never read an instruction manual ... ever!

So even though he didn't leave behind an instruction manual, he certainly left behind teachings, wonderful memories and an absolute legacy.

We love you Dad and promise to keep your legacy alive and well.

The result

I didn't get struck down for swearing in church but I did receive lots of very positive comments about the eulogy. What do you think? Did the stories create a connection for you? Would you have liked to have a beer with him?

When I shared it with Mum, she said, 'I am not sure you should say "bloody" so much in church'. I said, 'But Mum, I am quoting Dad and he did say "bloody" a lot'. I thought I should remove the word until Mum called me back a few days later and told me she had spoken to the priest and he was more than okay with me saying 'bloody' in church.

Why it works

I used a combination of micro stories to highlight the values Dad had. Each story demonstrated a value that I wanted the congregation to know about Dad. The stories provided greater insights than just stating the values.

That's a wrap

- *Stories make speeches memorable and personal.* Whether for a wedding, birthday, farewell or eulogy, weaving a single, well-chosen story can create humour, warmth and connection far beyond a generic speech.

- *Short, focused stories resonate with audiences.* Both 'Release Russell' and 'Should have gone for it' show how even a single anecdote, if relevant and entertaining, can leave a lasting impression on the audience.

- *Stories convey values better than facts.* For a longer speech such as a eulogy, use a series of micro stories to showcase certain values and characteristics and to create a heartfelt and relatable portrait rather than simply presenting a dry timeline of events.

- *Practise aloud and manage emotion.* Practising stories aloud before delivery helps manage nerves and emotions, particularly with speeches that carry personal significance, such as a eulogy, wedding speech or milestone birthday speech.

- *Humour, insight and authenticity matter.* The most powerful speeches are authentic, mixing humour and sincerity while reflecting the speaker's genuine connection to the person or occasion.

Stories in the written format

16

Many of the stories shared in this chapter have been shared in presentations, meetings or social gatherings but have also been shared in the written format, on websites, blog posts and newsletters.

My newsletters predominantly contain a story. Not every newsletter, but the ones with stories always result in the highest engagement. Take this one, for example.

Have you ever wondered why some people seem to have positive and exciting things happen to them while others don't? There are many things that influence outcomes for people, but I believe there is one common attribute for people who achieve their goals. They let others know what their goals are.

As you would know from my previous posts, in May I attended a conference in New York. It was the 50th anniversary of the International Women's Forum and every year they have a Hall of Fame. This year one of the inductees was Anna Wintour.

For those who don't know Anna, she is the global Editorial Director of Vogue and the inspiration for the movie, The Devil Wears Prada.

One of my colleagues, Sally Curtain, was very excited about this. Sally is one of the most fashionable people I know. She could walk out in a hessian bag and still look amazing.

We arrived a few days before the conference and Sally told me and a few others that her goal for the conference was to meet Anna Wintour and get a photo with her. The slight problem was that we didn't know if she was going to be at the conference to accept her award.

Sally kept mentioning it over the next few days so other people became aware of her goal. I told Sally that if it happened, I would take photos for her.

So, the night of the gala dinner arrived. We were all taking our seats when one of our colleagues said, 'OMG, Anna Wintour is here'. I immediately ran to Sally and said, 'The eagle has landed!' Sally looked over to see Anna just about to take her seat. She jumped into action, threw me her phone and said, 'Right, we're on'.

Out of pure adrenaline and excitement Sally made a beeline to Anna, which meant she was the first person to approach her. I made a beeline to the opposite side of the table and started taking photos.

Sally and Anna spoke for about a minute. Photos were taken. Life goals achieved. Mission accomplished!

Sally, who was beside herself, shared with everyone afterwards that she and her new BFF had hit it off. And that upon introduction (read: interruption), Anna lived up to her reputation and rather than saying 'Hello', paid Sally the ultimate compliment of looking her up and down...as only Anna Wintour can! (This could be a scene from the movie, people!) Under pressure, and without having thought about what she'd say to Anna if she got to meet her, Sally made the rookie mistake of asking Anna if she liked her dress. Rather than waiting for Anna's response, she composed herself and went on to promote the TAFE course she leads. She talked about their amazing sustainable fashion hub and program in Cremorne, Victoria. She finished by inviting Anna over for a visit!

If Sally had not made her goals known … if she had not put it out there and told people about wanting to meet Anna … then it may not have happened. In the now-or-never moment, those around Sally helped her pluck up the courage to actually do it.

What this reinforced for me is that if you want something and want it badly, you have to tell people about it. If you are keeping your goals to yourself, just in case they don't come true … guess what? They probably won't.

My advice regarding sharing stories in the written format is that they should be more succinct than if you were sharing them orally.

Wise words from Mum

Margie Warrell is an inspiring speaker and author. She has written several books on living bravely and her latest is called *The Courage Gap*. Margie is a fellow Aussie but lives in Washington DC and travels extensively for work. We met each other well over a decade ago and instantly connected. We are similar, both coming from large Catholic families with Irish roots.

Whenever I am in the United States or she is in Australia we attempt to catch up, but our calendars rarely align. The last time we physically caught up was when we both happened to be in New York and we could fit in a drink at an Irish pub (of course) before Margie jetted off again.

The following story is one she shared of her mum in her newsletter.

The story

Just before I began writing The Courage Gap *my beautiful mum passed away.*

There were countless times in the writing process when I wished I could call her. For encouragement. For her calming perspective. For the strength I'd leaned on since leaving home at 18.

Though I couldn't hear her voice on the other end of the phone, I could still hear her wisdom.

Two pieces of advice kept me going and I believe they may serve you, too.

1. *'Write to serve, not to impress.'*

   While she gave this to me as a writer, I believe it's a mantra for life and leadership. When I was caught in self-doubt and comparing myself and worrying I wasn't enough, her words pulled me back to centre. Focus on serving. Be brave. Keep going.

2. *'We all slip up. Be a little gentler with yourself.'*

   My mum reminded me, time and again, that perfection isn't the goal … progress is. Her voice encouraged me to offer myself grace.

   So if you've stumbled or fallen short lately, remember this: self-compassion isn't weakness. It's fuel to rise again.

   I hope her wisdom brings you the same comfort and courage it gave me.

   If you're navigating your own courage gap right now in life, leadership or simply within yourself, I wrote this book for you. If you've yet to read it, I hope its words will give you the encouragement to step forward a little braver than before.

The result

While writing this book and getting very close to submitting the manuscript, I received Margie's newsletter. So impressed I was by its succinctness and it insights I asked Margie if I could share it in my book. Her response: 'I'd be honoured. Am sure my mum would too!'

Why it works

This is another great example of words of wisdom not coming from the storyteller but through the storyteller via another character...in this case, Margie's mum.

My greatest inspiration

Jae is an engineering student and was part of a leadership program that I was asked to speak at. I spoke about my career and gave the cohort some tips on storytelling. Jae was inspired by what she heard and told me later that, 'It has completely changed the way I communicate. The biggest tip I learned is not to start a story with "Let me tell you a story"'.

Jae entered the following story into an International Women's Day writing competition at work. It's a great story and another example of someone else being the hero in the story.

The story

We often search for the perfect role model, someone who can inspire, motivate and challenge us. For years, I believed guidance had to come from someone official: someone with status or authority. But then, I realised the most valuable lessons often come from the people closest to us.

When I was in my second year of university, my mum told me she had also been accepted into university. I was surprised, but when she said it was something she had been thinking about for a while, I understood why. In the past, university wasn't common for women, and she never had the same opportunities as her brothers.

Studying as a mature student wasn't easy for her. I remember sitting beside her, teaching her how to navigate the university website, check her schedule and submit assignments, because she wasn't tech-savvy.

During her studies, she was also diagnosed with thyroid cancer. I couldn't understand why life had to be so unfair ... why it had to be my mum. Yet, she stayed strong and positive for herself and for her family, and today, she is in full remission, holding a bachelor's degree in Social Welfare.

She continues to march forward, now working toward her next goal of building a nursing home for elderly people who have no-one to rely on. Her commitment and resilience, despite personal and cultural barriers, inspires me to turn challenges into opportunities and stay true to my goals no matter the obstacles.

Looking back, I realise my mum was teaching me in the most powerful way ... through action, not words.

This International Women's Day, I honour the woman who has been the most inspiring force in my life, my mum.

The result

Jae didn't win the competition but she continues to share the story. She shared the story on LinkedIn and in other situations. Based on the reaction and comments she receives, she feels that through the story, people get to know her a bit better.

Why it works

This is another great example of the hero of the story not being the storyteller but a character in the story. When you share a story about the values of your parents, it reflects on you. It shows that you were raised in this environment and if you are sharing a story with pride, it shows that you also have the same values.

Traumatic life experiences

Tracey Ezard is a speaker, educator and author on all things leadership...specifically, what she calls Ferocious Warmth Leadership. Tracey has had two traumatic events happen to her over the past decade. One was while she was on a motorbike ride with friends, where two died in a fatal accident. The other was years later when she required open heart surgery. Tracey weaves both stories together to show her passion about what she does and why she does it.

Having two stories means you can use each one in isolation or combine them into a longer story.

This version of her story is on her website and she also shares versions of this story in her newsletter, her books and LinkedIn, as well as in her training workshops and keynote presentations.

The story

With what was to be one of the most traumatic and extreme experiences of my life in 2015, so too came my greatest learning.

While out on a motorbike ride with some close friends, two of our friends had a fatal accident. After an initial and hard grieving period, I jumped back into work using the things that were going well in my life as a distraction. I loved my work, I loved being a mum, I loved working with leaders and creating better workplace cultures.

So I decided that in this time of overwhelm I would be everything to everyone: family, friends and clients. But I wasn't being the person that I needed in that moment. I wasn't showing up for myself. For years after the accident, I continued to function from this space of putting everyone else's needs above my own. Over-functioning at its finest! 'I don't need help...I help'. As a result, my life began falling apart. I was exhausted, I was burned out, relationships started to crumble and I realised that despite doing good work, I wasn't bringing my best to my family, or myself. I realised this needed to change. I couldn't continue to limp along in life like this. Externally I may have looked like I was smashing goals, but internally I was struggling.

I made the decision to create a life that supported me. I needed to have the freedom to do what was good for me, not only what was good for others. It took a few years but I managed to develop the supports that I needed in my family and friends, in my business, in all areas of my life. I also learned how to give myself compassion and space to do the things I loved and fill my own cup. I then was able to live far more healthily and achieve goals more easily because, while I was still helping others, I was helping myself first. This came with an important lesson.

As a high-functioning person, the temptation can be to do it all yourself. But through this process, I learned that asking for help didn't mean I had failed and often I could do even better work and get better results if I did allow others to help. It pushed me as a leader to not only listen to my head (the results, the what I 'should' be doing), but also my heart (what is best for me and the people around me). I realised that if I wanted to continue to get better results, I needed to nurture my relationships. The relationships that fill me with joy, help me see what's possible, help me through tough times and help me to be able to give as well. Not only with others, but also my relationship with myself. I had to practise and fully embrace the role of ferocious warmth within my own life.

If you are a leader who is feeling exhausted and like you're doing it all yourself, I want you to know there is hope. You aren't failing, you are learning, and by allowing others to come on this learning journey with you, you are opening the door to amazing transformation and opportunity.

Another life-changing event for me came at the end of 2023. This solidified all of the work that I had done across the past few years.

In October 2023, I faced a major health challenge. But instead of my world shaking like it may have when I previously had to face life-changing revelations, I was able to take it in my stride. The supports that I had built into my life helped me to recover in a way that surprised me and my doctors. My mindset had shifted so that I was able to step into this traumatic space knowing that I would be able to cope. I had friends, family, colleagues and professional supporters who all showed up for me and truly helped me to survive a crisis situation. I was truly able to experience the power of the collective. It required me to be vulnerable and courageous and in doing so I was able to tap into immense wells of love and support. It reinforced what I already knew to be true about leadership, in a personal context.

In order to achieve peak performance in any area of our life or organisation we need to be balancing the head and the heart. We need to be equally focused on both sides of ourselves to get results. Our head gives us plans, strategy, logic, action; but our heart gives us connection, support and compassion. We need to have the ferocity to be living our purpose and achieve what we are aiming for, and the warmth and connection to bring others along for the journey. We need to be balanced in our approach. We need to embody ferocious warmth in everything we do.

The result

Tracey says that whenever she shares the story she receives some very positive feedback with people often sharing their own stories of grief. Even though Tracey shares the story to talk about her message of the link between your wellbeing and your leadership, the other benefit of this story is that it prompts people to get their heart health tested. Many have told her they undertook a coronary calcium scan thanks to her story and the tests showed concerns that needed to be treated.

This story showcases that stories can really inspire action and, in some cases, save lives.

Why it works

Tracey has allowed time to pass to ensure she has healed from these experiences before she reveals them. So, even though they are both traumatic events, you know that Tracey has survived and is okay now. This is important when sharing traumatic stories. Share stories of scars, not wounds.

That's a wrap

- *Stories are just as powerful written as spoken.* The written word, whether in newsletters, blogs, websites or LinkedIn posts, can evoke connection, insight and action just like an oral story.

- *Written stories should be more succinct.* While oral storytelling can carry more detail and pauses, written stories benefit from being tighter and sharper to retain the reader's attention.

- *Create once, deliver often.* A story crafted once can be repurposed across multiple formats, such as presentations, newsletters, social media, podcasts and speeches. Don't limit a good story to one platform.

- *Celebrate others as heroes.* Making other people the focus in your stories, as Margie and Jae did with their respective mothers, reflects positively on you while honouring others.

- *Stories can inspire action, and even save lives.* Tracey's vulnerability about her health experiences not only reinforces her leadership message but also prompts readers to check their own heart health.

Conclusion

My hope is that this book has given you insights on why stories are so critical and effective when it comes to communicating and influencing. I also hope this book has shed light on where to share stories and given you the capability to do so with confidence.

Ultimately, I hope it has increased your story intelligence so you can purposefully and skilfully use authentic storytelling to communicate with clarity and to connect, engage and inspire.

I encourage you to embrace AI and keep abreast of this evolving technology. Use AI as your creative partner to help you find and refine your stories. Let AI come along on the ride with you, but just make sure you never ever let it take control of the wheel.

AI may produce unlimited content, but it lacks the depth of human experience that makes your stories unique. In a world of distrust and fakeness, we are yearning for authenticity and your genuine stories might just be your superpower.

The next time you have to give a speech or pitch to a client, or provide a teaching moment to your child, ask yourself, 'What story will help me get my message across better?'

And please remember, storytelling is not about perfection... it's about connection.

Let me leave you with one final story (it would be rude not to).

When I left my corporate life back in 2005, I attempted to sell the concept of storytelling into organisations. As no-one was buying the concept of storytelling in business back then, I had a lot of time on my hands.

So with all this spare time, I decided to take up karate. I had always wanted to learn karate and with Alex and Jess being young girls I thought it could be fun for us to learn it, so I took it up.

Now, I am one of eight children and it would be fair to say I already knew how to punch. When I took up karate, however, I learned how to hold my fist the right way. I also learned how to use my hip when I punch and how to punch through a target and not at a target.

With lots of practice, practice, practice and refining my technique, now when I deliver a punch, it's a hell of a lot more powerful and effective than it was before.

I guarantee you the same will happen with your stories.

If you're prepared to practise, practise, practise and refine your technique, I guarantee your stories will be a hell of a lot more powerful and effective than they were before.

Connect with me

The best ways to get in touch or stay connected with my work are:

Podcast: Keeping it Real with Jac and Ral. Accessible via YouTube, Spotify, Apple, Amazon and wherever you access your podcasts.

LinkedIn: gabrielledolan

Website: gabrielledolan.com

Instagram: gabrielledolan.1

For workshop, speaking enquiries and corporate book sales, send an email to enquiry@gabrielledolan.com

Acknowledgements

I never know where to start when it comes to thanking people, but I suppose this time I should start with ChatGPT and Claude. Thank you for coming along for the ride.

In all seriousness, though, I feel this book is a compilation of my past 20 years. I also think this may be my last book on storytelling (never say never though) so I wanted to leave nothing on the table when it came to its content.

With that in mind, I would really like to thank everyone who has come on this ride with me. From clients I have worked with, to participants in my workshops, to audience members at my keynotes, to readers of my books and listeners of my podcasts. Thank you!

Also to my peers whom I have worked alongside at various stages over the past 20 years. You have challenged, guided and inspired me.

I don't want to start naming clients or colleagues because I know I will forget people so I will stick with the very cliché but true phrase of 'you know who you are'.

In regards to the production of this book, there are some people that need a mention.

Kelly Irving, my editor, who once again has made this book better. Thank you for your patience and insights.

To Lucy Raymond and the team at Wiley for believing in me as an author. Thank you for your ongoing support.

To Kieran Flanagan, who suggested the subtitle, which was better than all the AI generated ones … thanks for proving that human creativity can still win out.

To the people who took the time to rate the stories in the 'AI verses me' test. And to the people who submitted stories for the book. Even if your story did not make it into the book, I appreciate the support.

A massive thank you to the people who read the final draft and provided the testimonials that appear at the start of the book.

I would also like to thank Cancer.

Very early on in the writing process my usual mammogram revealed pre-cancerous cells that needed to be removed. The result was double breast surgery and missing the Kylie Minogue concert I was meant to attend that night … I don't know what was more devastating.

The operation meant that over the next few months, I was very limited in what I could do physically. Unable to do much more than write, having this book to work on kept me sane. So thank you Cancer for your perfect timing but you can now fuck off.

I would, however, like to thank everyone who supported me during that time and sent messages of love and support … again, you know who you are.

Of course, the final thanks to my husband, Steve, and two daughters, Alex and Jess. Thank you for being you. Love you … love you more.